Aboriginal youth and
the criminal justice system

Aboriginal youth
and the
criminal justice system
The injustice of justice?

Fay Gale
Vice-Chancellor
University of Western Australia

Rebecca Bailey-Harris
Department of Law
University of Adelaide

Joy Wundersitz
Department of Geography
University of Adelaide

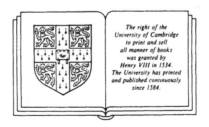

The right of the
University of Cambridge
to print and sell
all manner of books
was granted by
Henry VIII in 1534.
The University has printed
and published continuously
since 1584.

Cambridge University Press

Cambridge
New York Port Chester Melbourne Sydney

CAMBRIDGE UNIVERSITY PRESS
Cambridge, New York, Melbourne, Madrid, Cape Town, Singapore,
São Paulo, Delhi, Dubai, Tokyo

Cambridge University Press
The Edinburgh Building, Cambridge CB2 8RU, UK

Published in the United States of America by Cambridge University Press, New York

www.cambridge.org
Information on this title: www.cambridge.org/9780521125987

© Cambridge University Press 1990

First published 1990
This digitally printed version 2009

A catalogue record for this publication is available from the British Library

National Library of Australia Cataloguing in Publication data

Gale, Fay, 1932–
    Aboriginal youth and the criminal justice system.
    Bibliography.
    Includes index.
    ISBN 0 521 37464 2.
    1. Juvenile justice, Administration of —
    Australia. [2]. Aborigines, Australian — Criminal
    justice system. I. Bailey-Harris, Rebecca J.
    II. Wundersitz, Joy. III. Title.
345.94'05'088055

Library of Congress Cataloguing in Publication data

Gale, Fay.
    Aboriginal youth and the criminal justice system.
    Includes bibliographical references.
    1. Australian aborigines — Criminal justice system.
    2. Australian aborigines — Youth. I. Bailey-Harris,
    Rebecca J. II. Wundersitz, Joy. III. Title.
GN665.G34 1990   364.3'6'0899915   89-25157

ISBN 978-0-521-37464-4 Hardback
ISBN 978-0-521-12598-7 Paperback

Contents

Figures and Tables

Appendixes

Preface

This book is a study of Aboriginal youth and their involvement with the criminal justice system. The research owes its origins to the concern of Aborigines with the plight of their young people. Aboriginal community leaders asked us as researchers to find out 'why our kids are always in trouble'. They sought behavioural explanations for the high reported crime rates amongst Aboriginal youth. Another initiative came from Aboriginal women, the mothers and aunts of those so frequently detained.

Our study utilises the expertise derived from more than one discipline. It is an examination of the operation of the criminal process, rather than an analysis of patterns of actual offending behaviour. This was determined by the methodology employed: we utilised official statistics on juvenile offending, which cannot reveal more than the process whereby individuals and groups are selected for formal treatment by the system. Our data are unique in detail and comprehensiveness, enabling a more thorough and far-reaching analysis of the juvenile justice process than has been possible elsewhere.

We set out, without any particular doctrinal or political preconceptions, to examine the real degree of involvement of Aboriginal youths in the criminal justice system. Our methodology enabled us to go further and to seek explanations for the dramatic figures which our research revealed. The findings in this book speak for themselves and carry a message for all those concerned with the delivery of social justice to minority groups.

Our work would never have been possible without the very great assistance we have received from a number of people. First and foremost is the Aboriginal community itself and, in particular, Mr John Austin and Mr Brian Butler, who provided the motivation for the study. No less deserving of thanks is the South Australian Department for Community Welfare, which generously made the statistical evidence available to us.

Its Research Committee also provided a valuable forum for the preliminary airing and discussion of our findings throughout the duration of the project. Their suggestions have at all times been highly constructive. In this context, our special thanks go to Dr Andrew Duguid (Principal Evaluation Officer, Evaluation and Research Unit) and Mr Patrick Bradley (Projects Manager, Data Analysis Unit, Department for Community Welfare) for their strong and on-going support. We would hasten to add, however, that the analysis presented in this book and the conclusions drawn are entirely those of the authors and in no way reflect the views of the Department for Community Welfare.

Special acknowledgement is also due to the Aboriginal Legal Rights Movement, and in particular to Mr David Alcock, barrister and solicitor, who gave us invaluable advice on the operation of the Children's Court and willingly read and offered suggestions on various chapters in this book. His unstinting encouragement and perceptive insights have been much appreciated.

Numerous people within the University of Adelaide have given us both professional and technical support. Mr Errol Bamford, systems analyst, Department of Geography, provided invaluable assistance in organising and maintaining the massive data files for analysis on the University Vax. Mr Phil Leppard, statistical consultant, Department of Mathematics, provided much needed guidance regarding statistical procedures and undertook all of the data processing for the matched sampling and logistic regression analysis. To Ms Jo Gagliardi, of the Department of Geography, go our special thanks for typing the manuscript and then patiently retyping and correcting it on numerous occasions as our ideas evolved. Ms Linda Lambie and Ms Judy Smith of the Department of Law also assisted with the typing of portions of the early drafts. Ms Debra Cant, Mrs Chris Crothers and Mr Max Foale of the Geography Department undertook all cartographic work.

Finally, we thank the Australian Research Council (formerly the Australian Research Grants Scheme) which provided generous funding over a number of years. Without their support, the project would never have been undertaken. Additional support was also obtained from University of Adelaide Research Grants.

Fay Gale
Rebecca Bailey-Harris
Joy Wundersitz

Introduction

Aboriginal people have no reason to believe in the capacity of our legal systems to provide protection or justice, nor in the willingness or ability of the administrators of justice to act in an even-handed manner. As a result of European occupation of this country, the original owners have not only been dispossessed of their land but have also been mistreated by the very legal systems which were supposed to bring them enlightened forms of justice. Australia's adoption of British legal systems led to the false impression that justice would be administered in an equitable manner to all Australians. Yet the position of Aborigines before the law does not support this belief. In fact it casts doubt on many aspects of the judicial system as it operates in the lives of deprived or disadvantaged persons generally.

In two hundred years we have failed to come to grips with the essential causes of this injustice. As one Australian colony after another was occupied, official speeches full of idealism offered worthless promises to Aboriginal residents. In 1839, for example, Governor Gipps wrote:

> As human beings partaking of our common nature — as the Aboriginal possessors of the soil from which the wealth of the country has been principally derived — and as subjects of the Queen, whose authority extends over every part of New Holland — the natives of the colony have an equal right with the people of European origin to the protection and assistance of the law of England (Public notice of Governor Gipps, N.S.W., 21 May 1839).

The proclamation read by Governor Hindmarsh to establish the colony of South Australia on 28 December 1836 dealt almost entirely with Aboriginal justice. The same proclamation is still read each year with due pomp and ceremony on 28 December at the site at which it was first read:

> It is also, at this time, especially my duty to apprise the Colonists of my resolution to take every lawful means for extending the same Protection to the Native population as to the rest of His Majesty's Subjects and my firm determination to punish with exemplary severity all acts of violence or

injustice which may in any manner be practised or attempted against the Natives who are to be considered as much under the safeguard of the law as the Colonists themselves, and equally entitled to the Privileges of British Subjects.

Yet these first pompous speeches about British justice for all Australians were not translated into action, although their regular reiteration might give the pretence of their being so. Instead, injustice of the worst kind was meted out by agents of the law. Accounts of gangs of Aborigines bound together in leg irons, of children snatched from their parents, of families massacred, these atrocities are only now being brought into the open. It was the official protectors, the police, who were often given the task of rounding up Aboriginal groups and forcibly taking them to their destruction.

Whilst Australians are now coming to accept the injustices of the past, they are less willing to accept that a similar situation still exists. Yet past injustices continue, albeit in more subtle forms. Young Aboriginal men are still dying at the hands of the law, often in police cells for crimes which they did not commit or for behaviour which would go unmarked and unpunished if perpetrated by a white person. Much of the unjust treatment is unwitting or unintentional, done in the best interests of society and entirely in accordance with the law. But so were many past atrocities.

The reasons for Australia's abject failure to give British justice to Aboriginal people are still little understood. Research into Aboriginal entanglement with the criminal justice system in this country is still in its infancy. The area of juvenile justice, the focus of this book, has been almost entirely neglected. Yet it is precisely this area about which Aboriginal people are most concerned. The distinctive features of the juvenile system, with its structural alternatives to formal court procedures and its heavy emphasis on the rehabilitation of the individual offender, give ample scope for differential treatment. Furthermore, when young Aborigines are disadvantaged by their contact with the law at this early stage, serious repercussions are felt well into their adult lives. There is absolutely no doubt that such disadvantage exists and that its conse-quences are extremely serious — indeed, for some even fatal. In view of this, it is surprising that the little research into criminal justice which has been carried out in Australia has concentrated on adults. The whole process of disadvantage before the law has been set in train long before Aborigines ever reach the adult courts. Even to begin to come to grips with the problems of injustice to adult Aborigines or issues such as black deaths in custody, it is essential to study first the roots of the process, namely the differential treatment meted out by the juvenile system.

This book presents a thorough examination of the degree of involve-ment of Aboriginal youth in the juvenile justice system, using one State in Australia — South Australia — as the case study. The nature of the official data available in this State permitted an empirical study in a breadth and detail not hitherto attempted within Australia in this field. Whilst official crime statistics are not reliable indicators of real levels of offending behaviour, they do present an accurate picture of the operation of the official justice process and the treatment received by minority groups as they pass through it. It was therefore possible to monitor the effects, over the long-term and over a broad geographical perspective, of well-intentioned legislative and welfare reforms. The results were sometimes far from expected. In many instances the wording of recent legislation is not unlike the high-sounding moral phrases of the earlier declarations, and equally impractical in terms of achieving real justice.

South Australia has a long history of law reform in juvenile justice and is widely regarded as a leader in this field. This State was a pioneer in the creation of a separate system of juvenile justice for young persons a century ago. It was one of the first jurisdictions in the Western world to incorporate a welfare approach to the child, and it was also one of the first to question and modify it. Yet despite concerted efforts to improve the juvenile justice system in South Australia, its operation in practice for young Aborigines remains far from ideal. Moreover, the positive steps that have been taken to assist Aborigines, such as the provision of a special legal aid service, appear to have had little impact in reducing the degree of Aboriginal involvement with the law.

Aboriginal youth is over-represented at every level of the juvenile justice system throughout Australia, from the point of apprehension through the various pre-trial processes to the ultimate stage of adjudication and disposition. In South Australia, the harshest path through the juvenile system begins with a police arrest, followed by referral to the Children's Court, and culminating in a sentence of detention. The 'easiest' path entails being reported by police, followed by diversion to a Children's Aid Panel where, in most cases, a simple warning and counselling results. A far greater proportion of Aboriginal than other young people follow the harshest route. In other words, at each point in the system where discretion operates, young Aborigines are significantly more likely than other young persons to receive the most severe outcomes of those available to the decision-makers.

During the five-year period, July 1979 to June 1984, analysed in this book, some 43.4 per cent of young Aborigines who were brought into the system came by way of an arrest rather than a police report. In contrast, only 19.7 per cent of non-Aborigines were apprehended by means of an arrest, whereas 80.3 per cent were reported. Once in the system, almost three-quarters (71.3 per cent) of Aboriginal youth were referred to the Children's Court rather than diverted to Children's Aid Panels. The corresponding figure for young non-Aborigines was 37.4 per cent. Finally, at the point of disposition, the Children's Court sentenced some 10.2 per cent of young Aborigines to detention compared with only 4.2 per cent of other youth.

The disparity in outcomes between the two groups at the various discretionary points in the system is illustrated in Figure 1. As shown, Aboriginal youth were more likely to be arrested, more likely to be referred to Court and, once before the Court, more likely to be sentenced to detention than other youth.

As a result of this discrepancy in treatment at each level of decision-making, the extent of Aboriginal disadvantage actually increases as they move deeper into the system. During the period 1979–1984, members of this group accounted for a mere 1.2 per cent of South Australia's youth population. However, during that time they represented 7.8 per cent of all youth apprehended, 13.9 per cent of all Court referrals and a substantial 28.1 per cent of all detention orders. Figure 2 clearly illustrates this

(a) Proportion of appearances based on ARREST

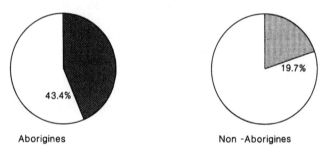

(b) Proportion of appearances REFERRED TO COURT

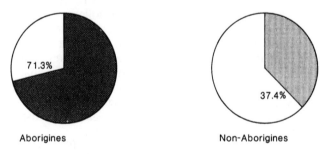

(c) Proportion of Court appearances resulting in DETENTION

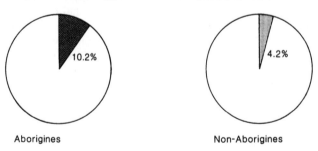

Figure 1: Comparison of outcomes for Aboriginal and non-Aboriginal youth at the point of arrest, referral to court and detention.

ARREST

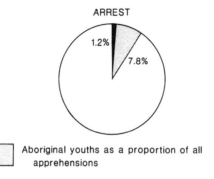

1.2%

7.8%

☐ Aboriginal youths as a proportion of all
   apprehensions

REFERRAL TO COURT

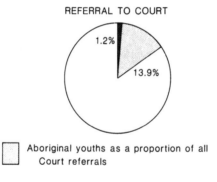

1.2%

13.9%

☐ Aboriginal youths as a proportion of all
   Court referrals

DETENTION

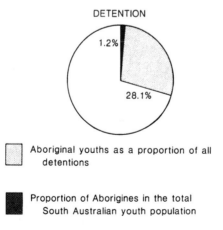

1.2%

28.1%

☐ Aboriginal youths as a proportion of all
   detentions

■ Proportion of Aborigines in the total
   South Australian youth population

Figure 2: Proportion of Aboriginal youth at each discretionary stage in the
South Australian juvenile justice system.

process of bias amplification as accused Aboriginal youth pass from one stage of the juvenile justice process to another. Primarily these are young Aboriginal males, since males outnumber females in all juvenile statistics. Nevertheless, the term 'Aboriginal youth' includes females as well as males. Although young Aboriginal women represent only a small proportion of the young Aborigines who move through the criminal justice system, they also are over-represented in comparison to young white women.

These statistics do not prove that Aboriginal youth commit more crimes than white youth, but they do raise the possibility that the law is applied differentially by law-enforcement agencies. The official crime statistics reflect the process whereby certain individuals or groups of individuals are selected for formal treatment by the criminal justice system. The essential selectivity of this process is both inherent in, and facilitated by, the element of discretion which exists at every level of any juvenile justice system. As two commentators in the United Kingdom have noted:

> The correlation between crime and disadvantage may well reflect the differential reaction of social control agencies (Freeman, 1983: 82).

> The relatively high concentration of socially disadvantaged children amongst identified delinquents may reflect little more than the selective attention that police officers give to deprived areas (Martin, 1982: 148).

These observations apply with equal force to the apprehension and subsequent treatment of Aboriginal youth in South Australia.

Although there is evidence that racial identity may play some role in the decision-making processes operating in the South Australian juvenile justice system, the explanation for the disparity in treatment accorded members of this group is by no means as simple as this. Class bias also seems to be operating, with certain groups in the broader community, such as the unemployed or those living in areas of lower socio-economic status, being singled out for consistently harsher treatment. The fact that Aboriginal youth are concentrated within such groups contributes to their different treatment. Numerous other studies conducted in North America and Great Britain have pointed to the operation of race and/or class bias in the way the law operates, and to that extent, this study simply reiterates such findings. However, what other studies have not generally demonstrated is that a decision taken at one level of the system can, in itself, become a crucial factor influencing decisions taken at subsequent levels. This book clearly establishes that the initial decision made by police at the very gateway into the formal justice system — whether to arrest or summons a child — has significant repercussions for the child's subsequent passage through the system. More specifically, the very fact of being arrested rather than reported by police proved to be one of the main determinants of a referral to Court, with all the negative consequences which that entailed. The fact of being referred to Court usually resulted in the young person's acquisition of a criminal record, which in turn, was a primary determinant of the Court's decision to sentence him or her to detention.

Consequently, the high level of Aboriginal over-representation at the ultimate stage of the juvenile justice process — detention — proved to be largely the result of a compounding effect of discrimination (both racial and class-based) suffered at earlier steps in the criminal process. Thus, as disturbing as are detention rates for young Aborigines, the problem of differential treatment in fact begins at a far earlier stage in the criminal justice process, and its effects are compounded as that individual passes further into the system.

These findings highlight the fact that any study of criminal justice must take a broad perspective by analysing the operation of the system at all of its stages, and not to concentrate, as most earlier studies have done, solely on its sentencing conclusion. As Feeley (1979) has argued, the pre-adjudication process may constitute the real punishment for the accused individual.

In *The Process is the Punishment* (1979: 241) Feeley observed that:

> Liberal legal theory directs attention to formal outcomes, to the conditions giving rise to the application of the criminal sanction of adjudication and sentence. Most social science research has followed this lead, searching for the causes of sanctioning at these stages. But this emphasis produces a distorted vision of the process and the sanctions it dispenses. The real punishment for many people is the pre-trial process itself . . .

In his study of the operation of a lower criminal court in New Haven, Connecticut, Feeley developed this thesis by examining the real costs to the accused individual of the pre-trial process, namely pre-trial detention, the awarding of bail, obtaining legal representation, adjournments, delays and pre-trial diversion. He found that (1979: 31–2):

> when we view criminal sanctioning from this broader functional perspective, the locus of court-imposed sanctioning shifts dramatically away from adjudication, plea bargaining and sentencing to the earlier pre-trial stages. In essence, the process itself is the punishment. The time, effort, money and opportunities lost as a direct result of being caught up in the system can quickly come to outweigh the penalty that issues from adjudication and sentence. Furthermore, pre-trial costs do not distinguish between innocent and guilty; they are borne by all, by those whose cases are . . . dismissed as well as by those who are pronounced guilty.

Feeley's thesis has a particularly poignant application in light of the current debate surrounding Aboriginal deaths in custody in Australia. Over one hundred such deaths have occurred in the last decade, many of them involving pre-trial remand in police custody.

The fact that conventional explanations for the extent of Aboriginal over-representation do not prove to be satisfactory raises an unpalatable question: is racial discrimination such an integral part of Australian society that no justice system can deliver equity to Aboriginal people? In saying this we realise that one of the major factors circumventing justice lies in the nature of the juvenile justice system itself. Discretion is an essential part of any such system. Yet the exercise of discretion provides the opportunity for differential treatment of racial minorities. The element of discretion is essential if rehabilitation rather than punishment is intended. In juvenile justice therefore, all agents of the law are given freedom to determine which measures will best promote the future rehabilitation of the individual offender concerned. Later chapters of this book, however, demonstrate that the exercise of such discretion largely determines the extraordinarily high incidence of Aboriginal youths being processed by the juvenile justice system. Whilst we would in no way advocate the removal of discretion from the system, essential as it is to the rehabilitative goal, it must be realised that the very use of discretion produces injustice. For this a remedy, however elusive, must be sought. It may be that the discretionary decision-making process reveals the profound racial biases endemic in contemporary Australian society, and that those biases, rather than the legal system itself, should be the target of future reformers.

This book, in taking a long-term look at the broad effects of legislative and welfare reforms, shows that the position of Aboriginal youth, far from being improved by such reforms, has worsened. Changes in the law and in the welfare structures, however well-meaning, have totally failed to improve the disadvantaged position of young Aborigines brought into the justice process. A major reason for this lies in the fact that the differential treatment experienced by Aboriginal youth is entirely legal and well within the guidelines of each sector of the justice system. This book shows that by and large, the decision-makers at each level of the system operate quite legally, even when being apparently discriminatory. In fact, a high proportion of the operators of the system go to extreme lengths to try to give Aboriginal youth a fair opportunity for both justice and rehabilitation. Most providers are extremely frustrated at their own inability to deliver equity to Aboriginal youth. It is quite clear that the roots of injustice lie within the justice system itself as much as with individual agents of the law. Therefore, because any justice system is a reflection of the cultural values of the society in which it operates, it is impossible to avoid the conclusion that the discrimination patently suffered by young Aborigines within the juvenile justice system, even one that is highly welfare-oriented, can be explained only by causes lying deep within contemporary society — the unacceptable face of social, cultural and racial bias.

If it can be proved, as our findings will suggest, that the justice system is unjust to visible minorities who are already socially and economically disadvantaged, then a formidable and urgent task lies ahead for future reformers. This is especially so since, to date, the numerous reforms at both legislative and welfare levels have apparently failed to deliver even the beginnings of equity.

1
Blacks and the Law

In the international field, the United States has led the way in studies of the disadvantaged legal position of blacks; so much so that a decade ago in 1979, Pope could give his article the title 'Race and Crime Revisited'. Studies such as those of Axelrad (1952) and Goldman (1963) first highlighted the differential selection of black and white youths for formal Court processing, and numerous researchers since then have provided ample documentation of the over-representation of blacks (and in particular, black males) at every stage of the adult and juvenile criminal justice processes. Nor is there any evidence from recent studies that the situation is improving, despite 'the revolutionary changes in race relations, brought about by the civil rights movement over two decades ago' (Chilton and Galvin, 1985: 3). These trends closely parallel those now being observed in Great Britain, where the post-war immigration of Africans and West Indians, coupled with the more recent influx of Pakistanis, Asians and groups from other Commonwealth countries, has now led British researchers to take greater interest in race issues generally, and specifically in the relationship between race and crime.

Yet, despite the wealth of information on the disadvantaged position of blacks before the law which has been available from overseas countries during the past three to four decades, concern in Australia over the plight of the indigenous population has been slow to gather momentum. It was not until the 1980s that studies of the disadvantages suffered by Aborigines in their contact with the white-dominated legal system became more frequent as evidenced, for example, by the publication of volumes such as *Ivory Scales* (Hazlehurst, 1987), *Aborigines and the Law* (Hanks and Keon-Cohen, 1984), *Aborigines and Criminal Justice* (Swanton, 1984), and *Justice Programs for Aboriginal and Other Indigenous Communities* (Hazlehurst, 1987). No doubt such studies will receive further impetus from the Royal Commission into Black Deaths in Custody. The *Interim Report* of this Royal Commission (1988), as well as the findings in specific cases, have attracted considerable media attention and, for the first time, has exposed widespread malpractices amongst a range of persons associated either directly or indirectly with law enforcement including police, prison officers and health workers.

Yet despite the growing body of descriptive or qualitative material now available, research based on the collection or analysis of 'hard' empirical evidence has remained slight. Hampered by the fact that most official crime records in this country do not record 'Aboriginality' (because, as one Queensland government official indicated to us, 'it would be racially prejudiced to do so'), the relatively small number of researchers who have sought to document the actual extent of Aboriginal involvement in the justice process have, in the main, been forced to engage in extensive field work or the equally time-consuming task of manually extracting data from existing police and Court files. These studies have therefore been restricted both geographically and temporally. As an indication of the sparsity of quantitative information, even in the one area where statistics are normally readily available — namely, imprisonment rates — it was not until June 1982 that the first National Prison Census was undertaken which provided a breakdown of the numbers of Aborigines being held as prisoners. Even the Royal Commission has been hampered by a lack of hard data. When it was first established, the Government was not even aware of how many Aborigines had died in custody since 1980. Initial figures were put at 44, but in the space of just twelve months, more than 60 additional cases had been identified. Nor was there any information on the number of Aborigines being held in police custody. In fact, the establishment of a data collection system to obtain such basic information became one of the first priorities for the Commission's research unit (Biles, 1988).

Yet despite this paucity of empirically based research, that which does exist indicates that, as in countries such as the U.S.A. and Great Britain, Aborigines experience disproportionate rates of contact with all facets of the criminal justice system. Elizabeth Eggleston (1976) was the first Australian researcher to document the inequitable position of Aboriginal adults before the law. She found that in Western Australia in the mid-1960s, Aborigines, who represented only 2.5 per cent of the total population in that State, accounted for 11 per cent of all charges laid. Her survey of ten Western Australian country towns also showed that Aborigines were more likely than non-Aborigines to be arrested (they accounted for 63 per cent of all arrests), were less likely to be released on police or Court bail and, once before a Court, were more likely to be sentenced to imprisonment (with 42 per cent being sent to gaol compared with only 19.6 per cent of the non-Aborigines). Partly as a result of this differential sentencing procedure, Aborigines accounted for 24 per cent of Western Australia's total prison population in 1965–66.

A more recent study conducted in Western Australia by Martin and Newby (1984) indicates little improvement. It was apparent from their survey of one metropolitan area and six country towns in that State during 1980–81 that the proportion of charges laid against Aborigines was much greater than their relative population size. In Wyndham and Halls Creek, where they constituted about 40–45 per cent of the population, Aborigines accounted for 83 per cent and 94 per cent of all charges respectively brought before the Criminal Courts of Summary Jurisdiction, while in a metropolitan area of Perth they constituted nearly 19 per cent of all charges but only 1 per cent of the total population. Moreover, once before the courts, a higher percentage of Aborigines received a sentence of imprisonment, compared with non-Aborigines. These imprisonment rates were augmented by the fact that 41 per cent of those Aborigines who were fined subsequently defaulted, compared with only 8 per cent of non-Aborigines who had been fined.

Similar patterns of over-representation of adult Aborigines have been noted elsewhere in Australia. In New South Wales, Milne (1983) found that, although members of this group made up only 0.8 per cent of that State's population, they accounted for 4.9 per cent of all charges laid in 1980. In the Northern Territory, where Aborigines represented one-quarter of the population, they constituted 78 per cent of all arrests during 1978 and 1979 (Ruddock Committee Report, 1980). In South Australia, Sutton and Koshnitsky (1983) reported that Aborigines were involved in 26 per cent of all arrests for minor offences during the last half of 1981, but constituted only 0.6 per cent of the State's adult population. These Aborigines were also less likely to receive bail than their non-Aboriginal counterparts.

In one of the most comprehensive empirical studies on Aborigines and criminal justice undertaken since the seminal work of Eggleston, the work of Cunneen and Robb (1987) provided ample documentation of Aboriginal over-representation in selected towns in north-western New South Wales. To cite just a few figures from this detailed study, they found that although Aborigines represented only 14 per cent of the total population in the surveyed area, they constituted 53.2 per cent of all arrests and 52.7 per cent of all Court appearances during 1985–86. Moreover, at the point of sentencing, 'Aborigines more often received a custodial sentence than non-Aborigines (7.8 per cent of outcomes versus 2.2 per cent)' (p. 116). At the other end of the sentencing scale, though, they were also more likely to have their charges withdrawn or dismissed; a finding consistent with the South Australian figures presented in this book.

The few other studies which have focused on adjudication and sentencing have also detected substantial differences in outcome between Aboriginal and non-Aboriginal adults. Collett and Graves (1972), in a survey of the rural town of Port Augusta, showed that whilst Aborigines accounted for only 5 per cent of the population, they represented 32 per cent of all convictions handed down by the town's Magistrate's Court. Chapman's (1976) examination of cases before the Port Adelaide Magistrate's Court in 1974 revealed that Aborigines were more likely to be fined but less likely to be given suspended sentences or released on bond.

Moreover, over 80 per cent of those Aborigines who were fined subsequently defaulted, which then resulted in a prison term. In contrast, only 10.5 per cent of whites who were fined then defaulted.

As noted earlier, the best-documented area of Aboriginal over-representation is imprisonment rates. Although such data provide only a distorted and incomplete picture of the criminal justice process since such a small proportion of accused end up in prison, these figures support the conclusion that 'Australia's Aborigines [are], if not the most incarcerated people in the world, then at least second to no other' (Clifford, 1981: 28). At 30 June 1986, Aborigines in Western Australia were 25.1 times more likely than non-Aborigines to be imprisoned. In South Australia it was 28.0 times; in New South Wales 17.0 times; in Victoria 17.1 times; in Tasmania 12.7 times; and in the Northern Territory 9.6 times. Moreover, a recent study of prisoners released from Western Australian prisons from July 1974 to June 1984, which was undertaken by Broadhurst *et al.* (1988), found that Aborigines, both males and females, were more likely to be reincarcerated than were other members of the community. They noted that 'the probability of recidivism for Aboriginal male prisoners was 80 per cent', compared with 48 per cent for non-Aboriginal male prisoners. Comparative figures for females were 75 per cent and 29 per cent respectively (p. 83). These differences applied irrespective of the type of offence committed.

While the number of studies focusing on the over-representation of Aboriginal adults is relatively small, still fewer exist in the juvenile area. Even information on the numbers of Aboriginal juveniles currently held in detention centres is extremely scarce. Only one State, Victoria, conducts a regular biennial census of young people held in youth training centres and reception centres which separately identifies Aborigines. In other States, information can be gleaned only from one-off studies or government reports such as those of Milne (1982) and Penniall (1982) in New South Wales, which focused on children in substitute care.

Milne (1982), for example, documented the over-representation of Aboriginal children in New South Wales corrective institutions controlled by the State Department of Youth and Community Services. He noted a steady increase in the rate of this over-representation since 1966. A similar survey conducted in Victoria by the Department of Community Welfare Services (1982) found that at June 1982, 8.3 per cent of all young people in that State's youth training centres were Aboriginal, even though they made up less than 1 per cent of Victoria's total population. A survey by the Western Australian Department for Community Services (1982) revealed that Aborigines accounted for less than 3 per cent of the State's population but 31.6 per cent of all children admitted to remand and assessment facilities from March 1973 to March 1974.

Information about the extent of involvement of Aboriginal children at earlier stages of the justice system is even more limited. In a relatively early Western Australian study, Mildern (1973) found that from 1968 to 1972 Aboriginal children were less likely to be 'diverted' to a Juvenile

Panel and were more likely to go to a Children's Court than were non-Aboriginal children. More recent data obtained from the Western Australian Department for Community Services demonstrate that this trend has continued, with Aborigines accounting for 25.7 per cent of all offenders coming before the Children's Court in 1985–86 but only 9.8 per cent of all children appearing before Panels. In South Australia, Sarri and Bradley (1980: 59) found that, from 1972 to 1977, Aboriginal youths on average had a combined Court and Aid Panel appearance rate of 440 per 1000 youths, compared with an overall State rate of 31.9 per 1000. Chisholm's (1983) study of all Children's Court appearances in the two New South Wales rural communities of Bourke and Nowra reported Aboriginal appearances to be five times greater than expected, given their relative population size.

Again, though, it is the work of Cunneen and Robb (1987) in the north-west of New South Wales which provides one of the most detailed breakdowns of Aboriginal juvenile involvement with the law. They found, for example, that during the 1985–86 survey period, young Aborigines accounted for 34.8 per cent of all cautions, 48 per cent of all citations (or summons) and 67.6 per cent of all criminal charges, and yet the authors estimate that this group accounted for no more than 15 per cent of the total population in the region. Moreover, as these figures suggest, the extent of this over-representation increases as the severity of the police response (from caution, through citation to being charged with an offence) increases.

The extent of over-representation of Aboriginal youths in the juvenile justice system in South Australia during the 1980s which is documented in this book is thus by no means unique. In fact, it seems to typify the situation in which Aboriginal youths and adults find themselves right across the continent. Why is this so? Are Aborigines, both youths and adults, more criminal than non-Aborigines? Does their apparent social and economic disadvantage result in them being singled out for greater notice by agents of the law? Or is the justice system discriminating against them on the grounds of race? To date, largely because of a lack of appropriate data, Australian researchers have gone no further than presenting a straightforward account of the extent of over-representation. There has been no empirical analysis of the reasons for that over-representation. Hence, determination of whether racial bias is a factor affecting decision-making in the criminal justice process has remained unanswered. Yet this question has received close attention from overseas researchers in recent decades.

In an attempt to explain the apparent correlation between race and crime, a spate of quantitative work emerged in the United States from the 1960s onwards which focused on the role of discretion and the relevance of race to judicial decision-making. Contradictory findings became apparent almost at once. Researchers such as Bullock (1961), Arnold (1971), Chiricos *et al.* (1972), Wolfgang *et al.* (1972) and Thornberry (1973) concluded that racial bias was present, whereas Green (1964), Terry

(1967), Chused (1973), Cohen (1975), and Petersen and Friday (1975) found no such relationship.

This lack of consistency in research results prompted criticism of the methodologies and statistical procedures used in these studies (Hagan, 1974, 1975; Wellford, 1975). Yet even the introduction during the latter half of the 1970s of sophisticated statistical procedures (such as discriminant function, multi-variate and log-linear analysis) which allowed for the simultaneous assessment of a range of factors, did not reduce the incidence of contradictory findings. Despite the plethora of studies conducted during this period (see for example, Burke and Turk, 1975; Hagan, 1975; Chiricos and Waldo, 1975; Lizotte, 1978; Hepburn, 1978; Farnworth and Horan, 1978; Cohen and Kluegel, 1978; and Elion and Megargee, 1979), no consensus could be reached on the relationship between race and judicial outcomes.

By the 1980s researchers in the United States had generally become reconciled to these contradictory findings, and a shift in emphasis emerged. Rather than trying to determine whether race bias did or did not exist, the issue became one of identifying those particular circumstances under which discrimination may operate to influence judicial outcomes, as opposed to those which preclude it. Thomas and Zingraff (1981), for example, stressed the importance of social context and noted that the importance of race to judicial decision-making could change over time, from one jurisdiction to another and from one level of decision-making to another within the same system. They also noted that the relevance of race could vary according to the relationship between victim and defendant. Similarly, Petersen and Hagan (1984) argued that the concept and relevance of race is linked to the particular social and historical setting in which it operates. It therefore changes both temporally and spatially, making apparently inconsistent research findings inevitable. In a study of police and court decisions relating to juveniles, Dannefer and Schutt (1982) specified 'some of the conditions under which bias may be expected', by comparing judicial decision-making in two counties which varied according to minority population size and degree of urbanisation. They also concluded that the decisions taken at one level of the system (in their case, police dispositions) could affect decisions taken at a later stage of processing, notably in Court sentencing, giving rise to what they termed the 'problem of "bias" amplification'.

In Britain, although a growing number of scholars such as Priestley *et al.* (1977), Bennett (1979), Mott (1983), and Farrington and Bennett (1981) have investigated the role of discretion, and police discretion in particular, in the criminal justice system, only a few have attempted to assess the relevance of race in the decision-making process. Moreover, the focus has been on the early stages of the criminal justice process. Stevens and Willis (1979), for example, considered arrests in the London Metropolitan Police District and found a disproportionately high arrest rate among the black population, which could not be entirely accounted for by socio-economic or demographic variables. Landau's (1981) study of police decisions regarding juveniles in five divisions of the London

Metropolitan Police District found that, in addition to legal factors such as prior criminal record and the type of offence, the police decision whether to charge the juvenile immediately or to refer him or her to a juvenile bureau was affected by the location where apprehension occurred and the youth's age and ethnic identity. Follow-up research by Landau and Nathan (1983) analysed a subsequent stage in the process; the decision by the juvenile bureau to caution or prosecute a young suspect. This revealed that, except for 'traffic' offences, black juveniles had considerably less chance of being cautioned than their white counterparts (p. 147), even allowing for a range of legal and non-legal factors.

In contrast, at the level of Court disposition, McConville and Baldwin (1982) found no evidence of systematic racial bias in the sentencing procedures of Crown Courts in London and Birmingham. A similar conclusion was reached by Crow and Cove (1984) after an analysis of outcomes handed down by juvenile, Magistrate's and Crown Courts in different parts of Britain. Both studies, however, noted the possibility that discrimination could have taken place at earlier stages of the criminal process.

In the light of these overseas findings, there is obviously a need for a better understanding of both the extent of and reasons for Aboriginal over-representation. Since virtually all available information shows that this minority group is disproportionately involved with the law, the general community assumes that this group is more 'criminal' in tendency, an assumption which reinforces existing stereotypes and racial prejudice. Aborigines also accept and internalise this judgement of themselves as inherent offenders. This in turn contributes to their already poor self-image and self-esteem. In fact, many Aboriginal families contacted during the course of this project thought it inevitable that their children would 'get into trouble', be arrested by police, come before the Court and end up in detention. Many mothers also assumed that death in a police cell was unavoidable for their sons. However, a substantial proportion of these mothers, whilst they accepted the inevitability of this, believed it was largely the result of unjust treatment by the law. Without a proper understanding of the issues involved, there is little chance that effective action can ever be taken by governments and others eager to remedy the injustices of contemporary society. Consequently, while almost all existing Australian studies have been content to present the degree of Aboriginal over-representation, this book takes the question much further. As well as looking closely at the extent of that over-representation, it also searches for the reasons behind it.

South Australia: A Case Study

South Australia provides a useful 'laboratory' in which to examine the operation of juvenile justice, because it possesses a computerised data source on youth offenders which, in terms of its size, continuity and separate identification of Aboriginality, permits a far more comprehensive study than has been possible elsewhere.

The ferment of social change which characterised South Australia in the 1960s and which led to a restructuring of juvenile justice that culminated in the passage of the *Juvenile Courts Act* (1971), had an important consequence. In the midst of the Social Welfare Advisory Council inquiry and the drafting of the new legislation, it was recognised that few quantitative data were available to assist in policy formulation. Consequently, with the creation of the new Department for Community Welfare and its expanded role in the area of juvenile justice, an innovative, computer-based system for collecting data on young offenders was devised to coincide with the commencement date of the new legislation, 1 July 1972. The aim was to provide a comprehensive record of all appearances taking place before the Juvenile Court and Aid Panels. To this end, some 130 or so discrete variables were collected for each appearance, and over the ensuing years these have been augmented and modified where necessary to accommodate legislative and administrative changes (see Appendix 1).

As with all crime statistics, the files are structured on the basis of appearances,[1] so that each appearance which takes place constitutes a discrete file case. However, the youth-offending files can also be analysed on the basis of individuals. As a result, it is possible to extract information on long-term individual offending patterns, and to determine whether, over a given period, we are dealing with a large number of once-only offenders or a relatively small number of individuals who are constantly being apprehended. Such information is obviously crucial in determining strategies for the treatment and rehabilitation of young persons coming before the juvenile justice system.

Apart from the sheer size and continuity of these files, and the availability of data relating either to appearances or to individuals, their importance lies in the separate identification of Aboriginal and non-Aboriginal youths. The inclusion of this racial identifier in the South Australian youth-offending files in 1972 made them unique in Australia at the time. In 1978 Western Australia began differentiating youth appearances on the basis of Aboriginal or non-Aboriginal identity, but the range of information collected was relatively limited. In 1984 the Northern Territory introduced a computerised data base on youth offences which also records Aboriginal or non-Aboriginal identity, but only for limited areas. New South Wales introduced a comparable recording system to that of South Australia in 1986. Within this context, the South Australian file dating back to 1972 is an invaluable study tool.

As noted earlier, because of the limited data available generally in Australia, most studies of Aboriginal involvement in criminal justice have been restricted in terms of locality, the range of information collected, the period involved, and the stage of criminal processing. In contrast, the data bank used here provides a unique opportunity to assess the level of Aboriginal participation at all levels of the juvenile justice process, both pre-trial and in Court, over the whole of South Australia and over a long period of time. This has made it possible not only to test for any bias amplification as individuals move through the various stages of the criminal process, but also to inquire whether one discretionary outcome 'impacts more oppressively' (Harding, 1985: 6) on the individual than another. It is of limited use, for example, to legislate for new sentencing procedures if the greatest impact and inequity occurs at the point of apprehension.

Yet despite the value of the data source, some words of warning must be issued. We are, after all, dealing with official crime statistics, the inadequacies of which have been well documented by numerous researchers and commentators. The most important and obvious of these is that official statistics reveal little about the real nature and extent of offending behaviour in the community. Instead, such statistics reflect only those offenders actually apprehended by police.

What crime is solved and who is apprehended is as much a reflection of the operation of the criminal justice process as of actual levels and patterns of offending behaviour. Certain offences may have higher 'clean-up' rates than others, thus giving the misleading impression that these offences are committed more frequently. Similarly, certain sub-groups within the community may be apprehended more often, not because they actually commit more offences, but because they are more visible and receive much greater attention from law-enforcement agents. Various self-report studies have indicated that although sample groups of black and white youths have, when interviewed, reported similar levels of offending or delinquent behaviour, it is the black group which comes to official notice significantly more often than the white group (Chambliss and Nagasawa, 1969; Hirschi, 1969; Williams and Gold, 1972; Gold and Reimer, 1975).

Because official statistics are limited in their ability to provide an insight into actual criminal behaviour, it has not been possible to determine whether Aboriginal youths offend more often or commit different or more serious offences than do non-Aboriginal youths. Nor do official statistics provide any information on what is arguably the most important decision taken by agents of the system, namely, the crucial decision made by police whether to proceed with the matter by actually apprehending a young offender or alternatively to administer a verbal caution only. Since police do not record such cautions in South Australia, there is no information on how many are administered or whether non-Aboriginal youths are more likely than are Aboriginal youths to be 'let off' with a warning. Nor is there any documented information dealing with the circumstances in which an apprehension takes place. There is a wealth of anecdotal material to suggest that Aboriginal youths are more likely to be targeted by police for apprehension, and there are numerous stories of what seem to be blatant discrimination operating against these young people at this initial contact point. However, official crime statistics provide no information on these issues. Data collection begins only after the young person has entered the processing mechanisms of the justice system. Consequently, in discussing the first crucial decision to initiate criminal proceedings, we were dependent on far less quantitative material and a vastly restricted coverage in area and time. A survey (Gale and Wundersitz, 1982) of some 200 Aboriginal households in metropolitan Adelaide, together with a lengthy period of street observations, provided a considerable amount of material. Yet, for obvious reasons, this information was primarily anecdotal or descriptive, and hence cannot provide a basis for broad generalisations.

Despite the lack of official information on the apprehension decision itself, the statistics do provide considerable insight into whether Aboriginal youths receive different outcomes from non-Aboriginal youths once they have entered the formal juvenile justice system, and more importantly whether the young offender's racial characteristics influence the decision-making processes operating at the different levels. Valuable as this is, this book has been able to go even further, and assess the interdependence between the various stages of the criminal justice system. The importance of this inter-connectedness is increasingly being recognised by overseas researchers. As Crow (1987: 311) noted recently, 'discrimination at one part of the process, direct or indirect, is likely to feed through to other parts and reinforce black people's perception of the whole system as racist'. By investigating such issues, this book is therefore able to ask important and sometimes unpleasant questions about the operation of the juvenile justice system. Hopefully, the analyses presented will alert legislators and administrators of the law as well as welfare service providers and the community in general to some of the inequities faced by Aborigines.

2
The Ideals of Juvenile Justice

Juvenile justice systems differ widely throughout the Western world, and even within Australia itself. In fact, Australia possesses no less than eight different systems of juvenile justice, with each State and Territory having its own legislation. Differences are not matters merely of procedural or institutional detail, but reflect differing concepts — for instance, the characterisation of a juvenile offence as a crime or a symptom of social dysfunction, or the relationship between punishment and rehabilitation. Yet despite their differences, most modern juvenile justice systems display a common characteristic: a far greater emphasis on rehabilitation of the individual offender than pertains in the criminal justice system as it is applied to adults. One aim of this book is to assess how young Aborigines fare in this system in which the State's intervention is intended to reduce the likelihood of an individual's re-offending. This chapter outlines the ideals of a juvenile justice system, in order to measure against them the realities of outcome for young Aborigines. South Australia provides an ideal location for such a case study since, as has often been observed, this State 'has long had a reputation as an innovator in its provisions for young offenders' (Nichols, 1985: 222).

Over many years South Australia has sought to improve justice for juveniles. In doing so it has not merely reformulated the details of legislation, but has also reassessed the entire conceptual framework upon which the operation of the system rests. Have such efforts at 'improvement' in fact achieved justice for young Aborigines? If not, could any attempts do so? The implications of these questions stretch beyond young Aborigines in South Australia and concern socially disadvantaged minority groups whatever society they exist within.

A separate system of criminal justice for young offenders, though now regarded as axiomatic, has a relatively short history in legislative terms.

The very first move towards a separate juvenile justice system occurred in England in 1847, where the *Summary Procedure Act* passed in that year enabled those aged under fourteen years accused of theft to be tried by magistrate alone (Parker, 1976). South Australia itself entered the field more than a century ago. Newman (1983) has described how the *Minor Offences Act* 1869 (S.A.) provided for summary trial of those aged under fourteen, and their discipline by parents rather than in institutions.

One of the earliest ideals of juvenile justice was the procedural separation of children from adult offenders. Behind this lay the motivation of protecting the young from 'contamination' through contact with more hardened criminals. South Australia's earlier steps reflected this philosophy. From 1890 all female offenders aged under eighteen and males under sixteen years of age were taken to the State Children's Department premises and were subsequently held there in a room set apart for that purpose. The Department's report of 1890 observed that 'the children are not in any way brought into contact with either the "lock-up" or the police Court'. The report of 1892 noted widespread approbation of the South Australian system in the international press of the day. For example, the *Child's Guardian* in London said:

> We give elsewhere an extract from the last report of the State Children's Department of South Australia, which we most earnestly commend to our readers . . . This colony has led the way in a departure which is alike in public interest and in the interest of justice to children.

Moreover, *The Philanthropist*, also published in London, noted that the Howard Association in its last report wrote

> This department [the State Children's Department of South Australia] at Adelaide has also made provision that juvenile offenders awaiting trial should not be kept at lock-ups or at police courts . . . Herein the colony is in advance of the mother country and of other nations.

This separation of the hearing of juvenile cases which had commenced in 1890 received statutory endorsement five years later with the passage of the *State Children's Act* (1895). Thus, although Massachusetts, U.S.A., is usually acknowledged as the world pioneer in establishing the first separate Children's Court in the early 1880s, it is clear that 'South Australia rates as one of the first governments in the world . . . to establish a Juvenile Court, and to provide special legislation for that purpose' (Social Welfare Advisory Council, 1970: 2).

To separate the juvenile justice system from the adult does not, however, conclude the question of what should be the conceptual framework of that system. Theorists and legislators alike have, over the years, been divided on one fundamental question: the appropriate characterisation of juvenile crime. Is the child to be held responsible for criminal behaviour and punished as such? Or is the criminal behaviour a symptom of social, personal and familial problems which require treatment? The first of these characterisations leads to the adoption of a 'justice' model, the second to a 'welfare' model. Public opinion and legislative enactments in Australia, Britain and the United States have over the years swung between the extremities of these two views.[1] The welfare approach adopts a deterministic view of criminal behaviour; its causes are identifiable and can therefore be treated and controlled. By contrast, a justice model is predicated on the conception of criminal behaviour as an exercise of free choice, which can be controlled only by a system of punishments which operate as deterrents.

Nevertheless, it is acknowledged that the conceptual dichotomy between the two is not entirely clear cut; social justice requires account to be taken of welfare considerations (see, for example, Lockyer, 1982). Moreover, in practice much legislation reflects a compromise between, or admixture of, elements from both models.

Chronologically speaking, recent Australian developments in juvenile justice have followed those in the United States, but only after some lapse in time. American jurisdictions were first and strongest in adopting a welfare model and subsequently, first to question and modify it in favour of justice considerations. The original concept of the Juvenile Court in the United States was a paternalistic institution, the proceedings of which were civil rather than criminal in nature. This concept was never fully accepted in Australia (Seymour, 1983: 186-7), where children's courts have remained modified criminal courts, as is true of England. A highly significant change of direction occurred in the United States in the 1960s, with increased criticism levelled against the Juvenile Court as an agent for welfare intervention. Much attention was focused on the procedural rights of young offenders, but substantive justice was also affected. The decision of the Supreme Court of the United States in *Re Gault* (1967: 387 U.S. 1) represented a landmark for future developments at both national and international levels. The decision was to prove, albeit belatedly, of direct influence in South Australia.

Gerald Gault, aged fifteen years, was taken into custody following a complaint that he had made indecent telephone calls to a neighbour. After hearings before a judge of the Juvenile Court of Gila County, Arizona, Gerald was committed to the State Industrial School as a juvenile delinquent until he should reach majority (twenty-one). This particular offence entailed for adults a fine of $5–$50, or imprisonment in gaol for not more than two months. Gerald's parents challenged the Juvenile Court's order, arguing that the Arizona Juvenile Code was unconstitutional and that the procedure used in Gerald's case constituted a denial of various rights of due process. Their challenge failed in the Supreme Court of Arizona, but succeeded in the Supreme Court of the United States. Whilst much of the decision turned on the particular legislation in question, the opinion of the U.S. Supreme Court contains a valuable and important discussion of general principle.

Fortas J. delivered the majority opinion of the Court. He highlighted the potential for deprivation of rights and liberty of the individual child in the adoption of a 'clinical' or 'protective' approach to young offenders. He stressed that young offenders should not, under the guise of the 'welfare' approach, be denied the fundamental protection of due process of law afforded to adults. In the United States, the report of the President's Commission on Law Enforcement and Justice, *Juvenile Delinquency and Youth Crime* (1967), followed the lead given by the decision in *Gault*, recommending that Juvenile Courts give more regard to the observance of due process. This report

> ... reflected a distrust of large-scale government intervention and a 'hands-off' policy was advocated, particularly where saving children from what was seen as the stigmatising and destructive effects of legal processing was concerned (Murray, 1985: 77).

This view is particularly relevant to Australia where the welfare approach may produce excessive intervention, particularly for those young people belonging to socially disadvantaged groups within society. There is no clearer example than that of Aborigines within Australia today.

Freeman (1983: 72) has drawn attention to the sharp contrast between developments in the United States and Britain in the 1960s:

> In Britain what counted for decriminalisation had reached its apogee (or nadir, depending on viewpoint) at roughly the same time with the Social Work (Scotland) Act in 1968 and the Children and Young Persons Act in 1969. It is astonishing in retrospect that nobody in Britain appeared to notice what was happening on the other side of the Atlantic.

During the 1960s in Britain there was considerable activity in the production of reports and government papers on juvenile justice.[2] The culmination was highly welfare-oriented legislation in both England and Scotland. The *Children and Young Persons Act* 1969 (England) has been described as 'the statutory high-water mark of a philosophy which puts needs before rights and treatment before punishment' and as a 'culmination of the child-saving, treatment-oriented ethic' (Freeman, 1983: 69, 77). Nevertheless, the more welfare-oriented sections of the Act were never implemented and the English system has retained a strong emphasis on accountability.

Scotland, however, fully embraced the welfare approach. The *Social Work (Scotland) Act* of 1968, which came into operation in 1971, is of particular interest in relation to South Australian developments at that time. The Act created the novel system of children's hearings in Scotland: replacing the court system for young offenders with non-judicial bodies consisting of lay members with power to impose compulsory measures of care 'in the best interests of the child' (section 43(1)). Children's hearings bear some resemblance to Children's Aid Panels created in South Australia at about the same time, although the South Australian Panels were never intended to replace a court system for young people.

From the 1940s through to the 1970s, South Australian legislation demonstrated an increasing adherence to the welfare model of juvenile justice; not until later was the force of United States rethinking to be felt. The *Juvenile Courts Act* 1941 (S.A.) required the welfare of the child to be considered in the making of any order. This approach was strengthened in the subsequent *Juvenile Courts Act* of 1965 which has been described as 'resting largely on the concept of the protection and welfare of the child' (Social Welfare Advisory Council, 1970: 2).

However, it was the *Juvenile Courts Act* 1971 (S.A.), which entrenched a welfare model of juvenile justice in the State. This Act stated that the interests of the child were to be the paramount consideration in offence-related and neglect proceedings alike (section 3). The Act was notable for the creation of Juvenile Aid Panels designed to reduce youth offences by providing an opportunity for constructive intervention in the lives of young offenders. Based on the premise that children are, by reason of their age and inexperience, not only less responsible for their actions but also more readily 'reformed' than adults, the Panels were intended to give the child and parents an 'early warning' of the consequences of further offending. Their basic function, then, was to counsel the child as to future conduct. The system's aims were clearly reflected in the statutory powers of an Aid Panel. It could simply warn or counsel the child and parents, or request either or both to enter into an undertaking as to future behaviour. The welfare input was to be assured by the Panel's composition — a social worker together with a police officer.

Henceforth, the concept of pre-trial diversion for juveniles took firm root in South Australia. Yet from the outset, Aid Panels were never intended to deal with persistent offenders nor with the most serious crimes. Diversion to such a Panel was restricted to those under sixteen years of age who had not been arrested. More serious cases went to the Juvenile Court, but even here children under sixteen years of age were not formally charged with the commission of a specific offence. Instead a complaint was laid alleging that the child was in need of care and control (section 42(1)). The casting of offence-related proceedings for younger children in this quasi-civil mould was unique in the history of juvenile court procedure in Australia.

That offending was viewed primarily as a symptom of underlying problems was further manifested in the orders the Juvenile Court of South Australia could make under the 1971 Act (section 42(2)). One option was for the Court to place the child under the care and control of the Minister of Community Welfare for a period expiring on or before the attainment of majority (section 42(2)(c)). The Minister thereby became the child's legal guardian (section 43). Under this legislative scheme, the Court itself was not empowered to fix the length of any detention period to be served. The way in which a young offender was subsequently dealt with, including any period of detention in a training centre, was a matter for the discretion of the Minister. In other words, there was no fixed sentencing by the Juvenile Court.

South Australia was not long in reconsidering its strong adherence to the welfare model of juvenile justice. In 1976, a Royal Commission was established to inquire into and report on, among other things, the administration of the *Juvenile Courts Act* 1971, and whether any changes by legislation or otherwise were necessary or desirable. Mohr J. was appointed Commissioner and his report appeared in 1977. The report reopened the whole question of the appropriate ideological model for processing young offenders. The Commissioner was strongly and directly influenced by the decision in *Gault*, which he considered

> points the way for the future by re-asserting the need for the protection of a child's legal rights, but also poses the dilemma of how this protection is to be achieved whilst still providing a distinctive system of criminal justice for children (p. 17).

Mohr J. posed the critical question: how to provide a special system of juvenile justice without eroding fundamental rights? He was thus fully aware of the potential for abuse of children's rights through the operation of the juvenile justice process:

> That there are children in the community who need help, encouragement and guidance is undoubted and programs designed to provide this sort of assistance are properly the province of a department such as Community Welfare. However, to use a system of criminal justice, modified at the disposal stage, and disregard the seriousness of the offence and prefer the social circumstances of the offender in deciding what course to follow after conviction is not to give the child more rights than an adult, it is to deny them (p. 78).

The Commissioner considered that the interests of a child under the criminal law necessitated the protection of due process. Moreover, he regarded the Juvenile Court as incapable under the legislation then in existence of discharging its duty to secure the child's future welfare, since the making of a care and control order placed the child's post-Court future under the discretion of a government department and the Court thereafter ceased to exercise any influence. The resulting *Children's Protection and Young Offenders Act* 1979 implemented most of the Commissioner's recommendations. Mohr (1977: 17) viewed his report not as a 'tougher line', but rather as giving children legal rights denied to them by the earlier legislation.

Fundamental to the 1979 Act, still current at the time of writing, is the separation of the criminal and civil jurisdictions of the Children's Court. The most significant underlying premise is that the commission of an offence is not *per se* to be used as the pretext for welfare intervention. The change in ideology has been reflected in procedural changes. No longer can criminal proceedings result in a care and control order with transfer of guardianship rights to the Minister.

Whilst the *Children's Protection and Young Offenders Act* 1979 represents a reaction in South Australia against the extremes of a welfare model of juvenile justice, it by no means constitutes an example of the pure justice model. Elements of the welfare approach remain integral to the current system. The prime example is the continuing commitment to the pre-trial diversionary system of Aid Panels. Indeed, the 1979 legislation extended the scope of these Panels' operation to encompass all young people under eighteen years of age and those who had been arrested. The assumed positive benefits of the Aid Panel system justified not only its continuance but its expansion. At the same time, a greater degree of refinement was introduced into the process of selection of cases for diversion through the creation of Screening Panels which operate as the crucial 'sieve' in determining the future course a case will take.[3] A further welfare element in the 1979 Act is the continued use of Social Background and Assessment Panel Reports submitted by officers of the Department for Community Welfare to the Children's Court prior to sentencing.

The sentencing principles applied to juvenile offenders under this legislation demonstrate how far it differs from a pure justice model, with the principles of sentencing remaining quite distinct from those applied to adults. As King C.J. observed in *Hallam* v. *O'Dea* (1979, 22 SASR: p. 136):

> There is no valid comparison between a sentence of imprisonment on an adult and the measures prescribed by the juvenile justice legislation. The Act prescribes methods of dealing with juvenile offenders which differ radically in nature and object from the methods used in relation to adult offenders.

For young offenders there is no fixed proportionality between crime and punishment, which is a hallmark of the pure justice model. The needs of the individual child are paramount in determining what measure will best effect his or her rehabilitation. The rehabilitative goal is expressly stated in the policy section (section 7) of the *Children's Protection and Young Offenders Act* 1979 (S.A.), which binds any Court, Panel or person exercising powers in the juvenile justice process. Punishment as retribution still plays no part in the sentencing of young offenders in South Australia. The underlying assumption, here as elsewhere in the world, is that child offenders have more potential for reform than their adult counterparts.

Moreover, the object is the prevention of future offending by the particular individual concerned; no element of general deterrence (of others) is present, nor does a simple tariff system of proportionality between crime and punishment apply. These principles have emerged clearly from case-law in South Australia as elsewhere. In *Hallam* v. *O'Dea* (1979), the Chief Justice observed that:

> In the case of an adult offender, the starting point will generally be the observance of a proper proportion between the gravity of the crime and the severity of the punishment. This fundamental principle of adult sentencing obviously has no place in fixing the period of detention under the *Children's Protection and Young Offenders Act* . . . (22, SASR: 134).

And again, in *R* v. *S., V., and Nates* (1982, 31 SASR: p. 265):

> The important thing . . . about . . . the Act is that it does not include the concept of general deterrence. Its impact is directed towards the individual child. Its purpose is the development of the personality of the child and his [*sic*] development as a responsible and useful member of the community.

These principles bind Aid Panels in the exercise of their powers under the Act, and indeed Screening Panels and any other law-enforcing agent involved in the juvenile justice process, whether at the trial or pre-trial stage.

Recent legislative developments elsewhere in Australia demonstrate an increasing consensus that the criminal jurisdiction of the Children's Court should be separated from its protective role exercised over children who are the victims of neglect and abuse. Recent legislation has been enacted in the Australian Capital Territory, in Victoria and most recently in New South Wales. It is notable that none of these new Acts create anything directly comparable to South Australia's Children's Aid Panels as a formal system of diversion, nor a formalised 'sieve' comparable to Screening Panels. Elsewhere in Australia, diversion of varying degrees of formality occurs at the police level. In other words, an institutional diversion system through non-judicial panels is by no means universal in Australia, nor, with some notable exceptions such as Scotland and some jurisdictions in the United States, elsewhere in the world. The obvious argument against Aid Panels is that they may draw more young persons into some form of contact with a formalised justice system than would occur if diversion existed only at the police level. At present the only jurisdiction within Australia with a system directly comparable to South Australia's Children's Aid Panels is Western Australia. These began operation in 1964 and were formally established by legislation in 1978 (*Child Welfare Amendment Act* 1978 (W.A.)). Their constitution and powers are identical with those of their South Australian counterparts. Yet Western Australia has not to date considered it appropriate to establish the formal 'sieve' represented by Screening Panels at the point of entry into the formal juvenile justice system.

Over many years South Australia has aimed to formulate the 'best' system of juvenile justice for young offenders. The recent emphasis has been on ensuring that children are not deprived of their rights to due process under the guise of welfare. Such reformulation has necessitated extensive reconsideration not only of legislation and its operation but also of the conceptual relationship between the individual's responsibility for his or her criminal behaviour and the State's right to intervene in the young offender's life in order to effect his or her rehabilitation. South Australia shares with many other juvenile justice systems the dual objectives of rehabilitating individual children while at the same time protecting the community from their criminal acts. Yet despite the spate of legislative activity concerning juvenile justice over the past two decades, South Australia is still not complacent about its achievements. In 1988 the Attorney-General announced a further review of the legislation governing the operation of Panels and of the Court on the grounds that there were still 'areas which had been causing concern' (*Adelaide Advertiser*, 8 March 1988).

This book examines how the juvenile justice system in South Australia, into which so much energy of law reformers has been channelled, operates in reality for young Aborigines. Does it deliver the justice it promises?

3

Welfare and Justice: Ideal Intentions but Differential Delivery

During the reforming decades of the 1960s and 1970s a spate of legislation appeared in both the juvenile justice and general welfare fields in South Australia. Underlying the program of legislative reform was the laudable motive of achieving greater equity for all members of the community. It also reflected a commitment to the notion that legislation is an effective tool for engineering social change.

Yet the various legal and welfare initiatives of the period do not appear to have made the system more equitable in practice. In fact, legislative changes have done little to improve the position of young Aborigines before the criminal law in South Australia. Not only has Aboriginal involvement in the juvenile justice system actually increased since the early 1970s, but at each stage of that system, this group continues to be singled out for harsher treatment than other young people. This remains true, even when Aborigines are compared with other highly visible ethnic groups. Quite simply, it seems that the ideals of legislative reform have not been translated into practice for Aboriginal youth. This suggests that legislation may not necessarily be an effective tool for engineering social change. In fact, there is evidence to show that the more attempts made to improve the delivery of justice, the more disadvantaged young Aborigines become.

The real effects of legislative reform undertaken in South Australia during the 1960s and 1970s were for many youths, and Aborigines in particular, quite negative. As each new piece of legislation was introduced, the net of social control was widened, with the result that ever-increasing numbers of children were brought into formal contact with the criminal justice process. In particular, there is some evidence to suggest that the introduction of pre-trial diversionary procedures, whilst reducing the number of children who were subjected to the stigmatising effects of a formal Court appearance, in fact also reduced the proportion of children who had previously been filtered out of the formal criminal justice process altogether, by means of a police caution or other informal treatment. The enormous increase in official contact with the criminal justice system, even at its pre-trial stages, raises serious questions of the social and economic costs involved to both the individual and the community. Furthermore, as Feeley (1979) has shown, any involvement with the formal process of the criminal law can of itself become a punishment.

A glance at Figure 3 suggests that the introduction of welfare-oriented legislation in 1965 had a dramatic effect on young people, bringing many more of them before the Court. This graph depicts the number of children and youths who appeared before the Adelaide Juvenile Court on serious charges or whose behaviour was interpreted as 'delinquent'.[1] In the

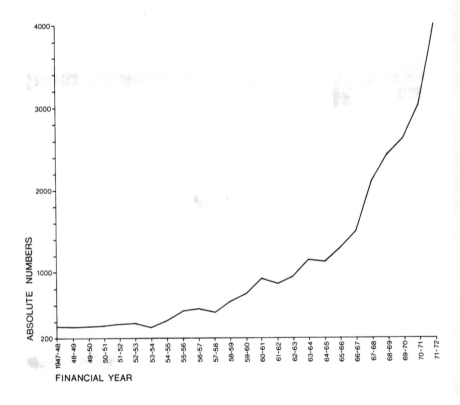

Figure 3: Number of appearances before the Adelaide Juvenile Court for serious offences or 'delinquent' behaviour, 1947–1972

eighteen-year period preceding the *Juvenile Courts Act* 1965, there was a steady overall rise in the numbers of youths processed, although annual fluctuations were evident. However, after the introduction of this strongly welfare-oriented piece of legislation, a steep increase occurred, which continued unabated over the ensuing years.

The introduction of Aid Panels by the *Juvenile Courts Act* 1971 seemed to cast the net even wider. This is illustrated in Figure 4, which details all offence-related youth appearances in South Australia. Sarri and Bradley (1980) attributed this sharp increase in apprehensions to a reduction in the police practice of cautioning youths, with police henceforth assuming that the newly introduced Aid Panels could deal with those first or minor offenders who had previously been the subject of such cautions. A similar effect — of bringing more young people into formal contact with the justice system — is repeated in 1979 with the creation of Screening Panels as the formal mechanism for determining a case's suitability for diversion. As Figure 4 shows, a further rise in formal appearances

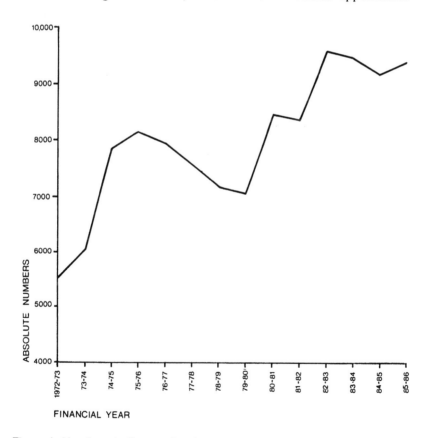

FINANCIAL YEAR

Figure 4: Number of offence-related appearances before Aid Panels and the Children's Court in South Australia, 1972–1986

occurred after that date. Furthermore, this legislation appeared precisely at the time when the system was beginning to settle back to a more 'normal' rate after the effects of the 1972 legislation.

It seems then, that a firm legislative commitment to the welfare of the child, together with subsequent attempts to refine the system by adding diversionary and pre-trial 'sieving' structures, had unforeseen negative consequences. Each new piece of legislation, rather than reducing the numbers of young people being formally processed, apparently contributed to a further increase. The following sections show that these various legislative changes had a greater impact on Aboriginal youths brought into the justice system than on their white counterparts.

Differential Treatment over Time

There are three crucial points within the South Australian juvenile justice system which involve the exercise of individual discretion: police decisions whether to initiate criminal proceedings and whether to apprehend by way of an arrest or a report; the referral decisions of Screening Panels; and Children's Court sentences (see Figure 5 for a simplified flow diagram). At all of these three stages Aboriginal and non-Aboriginal youths experience different outcomes; moreover, the treatment of Abor · igines has shown no improvement over the past fifteen years.

At the crucial point of entry into the system, substantial differences exist between Aborigines and other youths. According to the 1986 census, Aborigines represented only 1.7 per cent of the total youth

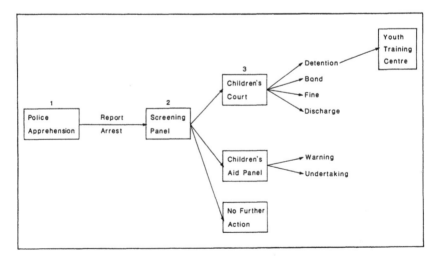

Figure 5: Schematic representation of the South Australian juvenile justice system, showing the major points at which discretion operates

population in South Australia but for the year ending 30 June 1986 they accounted for 9.3 per cent of all appearances before Aid Panels and the Children's Court. Thus the rate of appearance for Aboriginal youths was 164.0 per 1000 population. The corresponding rate for non-Aboriginal youths was only 27.2 appearances per 1000 population. This obvious disparity between the two groups has become exacerbated over time. Although the total number of appearances by young persons has increased substantially during the past two decades, the increase has been far more pronounced for Aborigines than for other youths. Between 1972–73 and 1985–86, there was a 111.0 per cent increase in the actual number of offence-related appearances by Aborigines. During the same period, appearances involving non-Aboriginal youths rose by 65.2 per cent.

Once police have determined to proceed with a matter, they must then decide on the method of apprehension; that is, whether to arrest the alleged offender or file a report, which subsequently results in the issuing of a summons or notice. Again, differences between the two groups are immediately apparent. Aborigines are much more likely to be arrested than are non-Aborigines. During the year ending 30 June 1986, 29.5 per cent of all Aboriginal appearances were based on arrest, compared with 12.8 per cent of all non-Aboriginal appearances. On a per capita basis, for every 1000 young Aborigines, 48.3 arrests took place, compared with only 3.5 arrests per 1000 non-Aboriginal youth.

In recent years there has been a general reduction in the use of arrest by police as a means of apprehension; but whilst this has led to an overall improvement for youth generally, the relative position of Aboriginal youths has deteriorated. In 1972–73, young Aborigines accounted for 10.6 per cent of all appearances brought about by way of arrest, but by 1985–86 this had risen to 19.0 per cent.

At the next discretionary stage in the system, Screening Panels decide the procedural future of a case; principally, whether the matter is to be referred to a Children's Aid Panel or be sent for trial before the Children's Court. An appearance before a non-judicial, informally structured Aid Panel represents a far less serious outcome for the individual than does a formal appearance before the Court. Not only is a Court hearing more stigmatising than an appearance before an Aid Panel, but the Court, unlike a Panel, is empowered to impose conventional penalties. Aborigines once again seem to be disadvantaged by this referral process. Screening Panels are far more likely to send Aboriginal youths to Court rather than divert them to Aid Panels. In 1985–86, 59.4 per cent of all Aboriginal cases were referred to the Children's Court, compared with 38.2 per cent of all non-Aboriginal appearances. On a per capita basis, the Court appearance rate for Aboriginal youth in that year was 97.5 per 1000 youth population, compared with only 10.4 per 1000 for non-Aboriginal youth. Moreover, as was the case with arrests, the relative disadvantage of Aboriginal youth at the point of referral has deteriorated over time. In 1979–80 when Screening Panels first came into operation, this group accounted for 11.7 per cent of all Children's Court appearances; by 1985–86 the figure had risen to 13.7 per cent.

The ultimate stage of the juvenile justice process is sentencing by the Children's Court, and the most serious penalty which can be imposed is detention. Although only a very small proportion of appearances by either group culminated in such an order, differences between Aborigines and other young people are again evident. In 1985–86, some 7.8 per cent of Aboriginal appearances before the Court resulted in detention (actual or suspended) compared with only 4.5 per cent of non-Aboriginal Court appearances. On a per capita basis, the rate of detention for Aboriginal youths was 7.6 per 1000, compared with a rate of only 0.5 per 1000 for non-Aboriginal youths. Yet, despite these large differences, the situation for young Aborigines in 1985–86 was actually the best it had been since the current legislation was enacted. In fact, in 1979–80 Aborigines accounted for 29.1 per cent of all detention orders but by 1985–86 this had declined to 21.4 per cent. It seems then, that in this one area, the disparity in outcomes between the two groups is narrowing. This is in stark contrast to the deteriorating situation of Aborigines at all other discretionary levels, and has been achieved only by a conscious determination on the part of judges in the Children's Court to keep young Aborigines out of detention for as long as possible.

Comparison with Other Ethnic Groups

The marked over-representation of Aboriginal youth in the juvenile justice system is not characteristic of other ethnically distinct groups, as would be expected if high visibility or cultural distinctiveness played a major part in bringing youths to the notice of agents of the juvenile justice system. When figures for each group are compared with the relative population size of that group, two factors become evident; firstly, Aborigines experience far greater disadvantage at each level of the system than do any other group of young people and secondly, the extent of Aboriginal disadvantage vis-à-vis that of other groups becomes more pronounced as individuals move through each successive stage of the system.

The ensuing discussion is based on the summation of five years of data, June 1979 to July 1984, following the inception of the *Children's Protection and Young Offenders Act*. By combining a number of years, an average picture emerges which gives a more accurate presentation of the situation than does a single year of data which may be subject to fluctuations.

Table 3.1 shows the extent of over- (or under-) representation of each birthplace group at four stages in the juvenile justice system. These were calculated using relative population figures as the baseline. For example, young people born in the United Kingdom accounted for 8.2 per cent of all youth in South Australia aged between ten and seventeen. This same group represented 9.0 per cent of all apprehensions. As a result, their rate of representation at the point of apprehension is 1.1 times greater than

Table 3.1:   Proportion of Aboriginal youth in the juvenile justice system, compared with other ethnic groups defined by birthplace

Birthplace	Proportion of population aged 10–17 years %	Extent of over- (under-) representation of each group		
		Apprehension	Arrest	Court referral	Detention
Australia (Aboriginal)	1.2	6.5	19.1	11.6	23.4
Australia (white)	86.5	−1.1	−1.3	−1.3	−1.8
United Kingdom	8.2	1.1	1.0	1.1	−1.3
Greece	0.2	1.5	1.5	1.5	2.5
Italy	0.4	−1.3	−1.3	−1.3	*
Other European	1.2	1.0	1.2	1.1	−1.2
Asian	1.1	−2.7	−5.5	−5.5	−2.7
Other	1.2	1.5	1.2	1.4	1.2
TOTAL	100.0				
	n=180,340	n=36,363	n=5969	n=11,603	n=574

*No Italian youths were sentenced to detention.

their relative population size. In this table, a group which records a representational ratio of 1.0 is neither under- nor over-represented but is being treated exactly according to the proportion of the total youth population they account for. Population figures drawn from the 1981 census are used for comparative purposes because they represent the mid-point of the five-year study period.

At the point of apprehension, where police decide whether or not to initiate criminal proceedings, the extent of Aboriginal over-representation is far more pronounced than that recorded for any other ethnic group. Young people born in the United Kingdom, Greece and 'other' countries (mainly New Zealand and the United States) are also over-represented, but only very slightly. Greek youths, for example, accounted for 0.3 per cent of all apprehensions, but constituted only 0.2 per cent of the total youth population. Their rate of representation was therefore 1.5 times greater than expected — a figure which is substantially lower than the figure of 6.5 recorded for Aborigines. In contrast, young people born in Australia, Italy and Asia are actually under-represented; that is, fewer are apprehended than expected, given their relative population size. The greatest under-representation is recorded by Asian youth. They accounted for 1.1 per cent of the youth population, but only 0.4 per cent of all apprehensions. Their level of participation at the point of entry was therefore 2.7 times lower than anticipated. Yet, like Aborigines they are highly distinctive both physically and culturally.

A similar pattern emerges when the method of apprehension (i.e. arrest or report) is examined. As the 'arrest' column in Table 3.1 shows, Aboriginal youth is even more out of line here than in the overall rate of apprehension. Young Aborigines were arrested 19.1 times more often than their relative population size would lead one to expect. Comparing their situation with those of other visible and culturally distinct ethnic groups, their arrest rate is astonishingly high. In fact, Asian youth, whom one might expect to be as visible as Aborigines, recorded the lowest proportion of arrests per head of population of any of the groups considered. They constituted 1.1 per cent of the population in South Australia aged 10–17 years, 0.4 per cent of all apprehensions and only 0.2 per cent of all arrest-based appearances. Thus, relative to their apprehension rate of 0.4 per cent, their rate of representation in arrest figures was two times lower than expected, but relative to their population size, it was 5.5 times lower. Of the other groups tested, Greeks and other Europeans were slightly over-represented while in contrast, those born in Australia and Italy were under-represented. The proportion of arrests ascribed to young people from the United Kingdom virtually equalled their proportion in the population, indicating that they were neither under- nor over-represented in the arrest figures.

An analysis of referrals by Screening Panels to the Children's Court shows that Aborigines are once again disadvantaged in comparison with other ethnic groups. Using relative population figures as the baseline, Aboriginal youth are referred to Court almost twelve times more often than expected. Of the other groups considered, the largest over-representation was recorded by the Greeks, but this was only 1.5 times greater than expected. Again, Asian youth were the most under-represented.

At the sentencing stage, Aboriginal youth are substantially disadvantaged in the very high proportions who receive detention: 23.4 times higher than expected. The only other groups to be over-represented at this final stage are the Greeks and (to a lesser extent) those from 'other' countries. Yet their disproportionate rate of detention was insignificant compared with that of Aborigines. Once again, it was the Asian-born youth who, on a per capita basis, were least likely to be sentenced to detention.

The inequitable position of Aborigines and the way in which their differential treatment is compounded at each stage of the juvenile justice system is illustrated graphically in Figure 6. In this diagram, those ethnic groups which are over-represented are shown above the baseline of 1.0, while those which are under-represented are located below the line. Not only do Aborigines start off in a worse position than other groups at the point of entry into the system, but their relative position deteriorates dramatically as they move through its subsequent stages. In fact, in terms of their population size, their rate of representation was 6.5 times higher at the point of entry, 11.6 times higher at the Court level and 23.4 times higher in terms of the numbers sentenced to detention.

The trend for white Australian-born youth is in direct contrast to that observed for Australian Aborigines. They are under-represented at each discretionary point, and this under-representation becomes more pronounced as they move through the system. At the point of entry, their rate of apprehension is 1.1 times lower than expected; at the Court referral

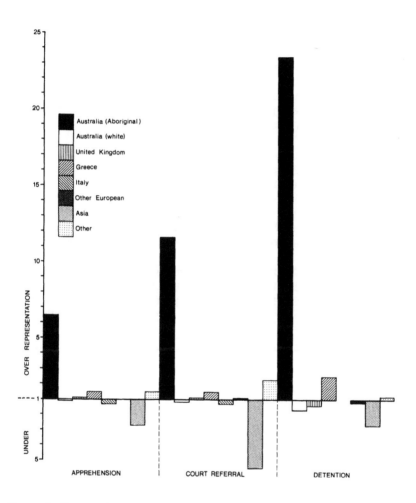

Figure 6: Extent of Aboriginal over-representation compared with other ethnic groups at the point of apprehension, Court referral and detention

level it is 1.3 times lower and when the detention stage is reached it is 1.8 times below that which would be expected. Asian-born youth, who at each stage exhibit the lowest rate of involvement of all groups, have a rate of representation which is the same at both the beginning and the end of the system: namely, 2.7 times lower than expected on a per capita basis. The pattern is clear: Aboriginal youth receives harsher outcomes, even when compared with other visible and culturally distinctive minority groups in the community.

Differential Treatment over Space

If the justice system operated equitably across the State, then population size should determine the proportion of Aborigines recorded in the crime statistics. This is not so. There are enormous geographical variations in the position of young Aborigines before the law across the State. Their degree of over-representation varies dramatically from one region to another and also, on a smaller scale, from suburb to suburb in the capital city of Adelaide.

In the ensuing discussion, the State has been divided into eight regions (see Figure 7) based on those used in the census. Although South Australia is being used as a case study, there is no reason to assume that the situation in this State is unique. At the main discretionary stages of the juvenile justice system, namely apprehension, arrest, referral to Court and sentence to detention, there is no clear relationship between the relative size of the Aboriginal population and their extent of over-representation in a given region.

At the apprehension stage, the degree of Aboriginal over-representation varies from 3.0 times in Outer Adelaide and the remote areas of South Australia to 22.6 times in the rural area designated as the Lower North–Yorke Peninsula region. Table 3.2 shows that Aboriginal over-representation in

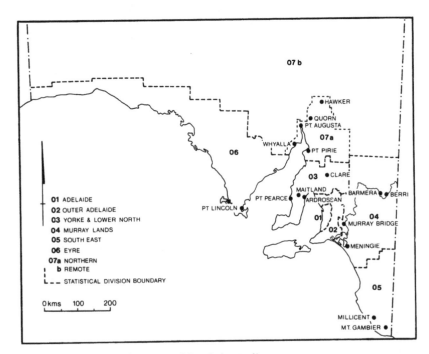

Figure 7: Statistical divisions of South Australia

arrest figures varied from 3.9 times in the remote areas of the State to an overwhelming value of 76.3 in the Lower North–Yorke Peninsula district. In both Eyre Peninsula and Northern South Australia, Aborigines account for approximately similar proportions of the population, yet they feature in 80.1 per cent of all arrest-based appearances in Eyre Peninsula but only 24.6 per cent of all such appearances in Northern South Australia. These figures inevitably produce large disparities between the two geographical regions in the degree of Aboriginal over-representation in arrests, namely 21.6 and 9.5 respectively.

Aboriginal over-representation before the Children's Court also exhibits enormous spatial variation. Aboriginal youths living in the Lower North–Yorke Peninsula region appeared before the Court 46.5 times more often than might be expected. In contrast, in the remote region of South Australia, Aboriginal representation before the Children's Court was only 3.7 times greater than their population numbers would predict.

The same pattern emerges at the sentencing stage. When compared with their relative population numbers, Aboriginal representation in detention orders is only 4.5 times greater than expected in the remote areas of the State, but is 46.8 times greater than anticipated in Adelaide, and a massive 102.3 times greater in the Lower North–Yorke Peninsula region.

Marked differences also occur on a smaller scale between towns, and once again, the relative size of the Aboriginal population does not seem to be a relevant factor. For example, two towns in the south-east of the

Table 3.2: Geographical variations in the extent of Aboriginal over-representation

Statistical Division	Aborigines as % of total population* per division, 1981 census %	Extent of over-representation of each group			
		Apprehension	Arrest	Court referral	Detention
Adelaide	0.4	10.3	26.0	20.3	46.8
Outer Adelaide	0.2	3.0	14.0	4.0	71.5
Lower North–Yorke Pen.	0.8	22.6	76.3	46.5	102.3
Murray Lands	1.3	15.7	42.0	23.9	56.1
South East	0.3	8.7	18.7	15.3	34.3
Eyre Peninsula	3.7	13.7	21.6	18.3	21.2
Northern S.A.	2.6	5.4	9.5	7.3	10.9
Remote S.A.	20.3	3.0	3.9	3.7	4.5

*These figures were derived from Table 4, p. 10, *Aboriginals in South Australia: a statistical profile*, Aust. Bureau of Statistics, Cat. No. 3205.4. It should be noted that they refer to total population figures and not just to the 10–17-year-olds because it was not possible to obtain Aboriginal age breakdowns for each of the statistical divisions. The degree of over-representation shown will thus differ slightly from that which would result had we been able to control for age.

State, Millicent and Mount Gambier, had the same proportion of Aborigines in their population: 0.3 per cent. Yet, Aboriginal representation at the point of apprehension was 20.7 times greater than expected at Millicent but only 7.0 times greater than expected at Mount Gambier. To take another example, in the two towns of Port Pirie and Port Augusta which, like Millicent and Mount Gambier, are close to each other, the extent of Aboriginal over-representation at the point of apprehension was approximately the same, namely 5.9 and 6.0 respectively. Yet in Port Pirie, Aborigines accounted for 0.3 per cent of the total population whereas in Port Augusta, they constituted a relatively high 7.3 per cent of the population.

Discrepancies between regions were also evident in relation to arrest figures. For instance, whilst Whyalla and Murray Bridge have approximately the same proportion of Aborigines in their total population (1.1 per cent and 1.6 per cent respectively), Aboriginal representation in the arrest figures is 8.2 times greater than expected at Whyalla but 29.5 times greater than expected at Murray Bridge. Similar variations were evident in relation to Court referral and detention rates.

Given the fact that population size does not appear to be relevant, one possible explanation for these geographical variations is that the pattern of Aboriginal offending behaviour itself varies geographically, with different environments providing different opportunities to engage in crime. Such a thesis is difficult to substantiate, especially since it cannot explain why Aboriginal youths living under similar conditions in neighbouring rural communities experience different rates of apprehension, arrest, Court referral and detention.

A more probable explanation lies in regional differences in the administration of juvenile justice. The highly discretionary nature of that system militates against its standardised operation over a wide geographical area where many individuals are involved. A clear example occurred recently in a town on the west coast of South Australia. In previous years, police in this town had notified community welfare workers of cases which needed to be screened only shortly before the Screening Panel met. This meant that community welfare workers were rarely prepared and had to rely heavily on police records and referral recommendations. At the instigation of a newly appointed Department for Community Welfare officer, a new policy was implemented whereby police were required to provide welfare workers with a list of cases at least two hours before a Screening Panel was convened. This, according to the officer, gave his staff more time to check any files or records held on the youth(s) in question, which put them in a more informed position during the screening process. Combined with this was a decision on the part of the welfare officers to recommend an Aid Panel appearance in as many cases as possible, even when the child was on a suspended sentence. Other practices were also instituted at this office, including the refusal to conduct screenings by phone, which had frequently occurred in the past; the refusal to conduct more than four Children's Aid Panel hearings in a given day in order to provide sufficient time between meetings to discuss each case; and the refusal to conduct any Aid Panel hearing concerning Aboriginal youth if an Aboriginal worker was not present. These relatively simple changes to administrative procedures resulted in a dramatic reduction in the percentage of Aborigines in this area who were referred to Court: from 82 per cent in 1985 to 32 per cent in 1986. Perhaps even more significant is the fact that such changes could be brought about by the determination of a single officer.

If individual police and welfare workers can produce positive results in the treatment of Aboriginal youth by relatively simple procedural changes, the reverse can also happen. Workers can be strongly influenced by community expectations, especially in small rural centres where they face social ostracism if they do not conform. In one town, for example, a police officer arrived with strongly supportive attitudes towards Aborigines. However, after a period of virtual persecution by townspeople which took the form of ostracism of his wife and exclusion of his children from sports groups, he adopted the popular stand and began to arrest, rather than caution, young Aborigines. His acceptance in the community rapidly improved, but Aboriginal crime statistics for the town increased considerably. It may, therefore, be no coincidence that the disadvantage experienced by Aboriginal youth is greatest in regions where prejudice against the local Aboriginal community is notoriously high.

Discretion is thus a two-edged sword. Depending on the attitudes and understanding of individual workers and the communities in which they live, it can operate to the benefit or detriment of Aboriginal young offenders. Police and welfare workers are inevitably limited not only by their own attitudes but also by those of the community in which they operate.

Lack of facilities in remote areas may contribute to regional variations in justice delivery, although not necessarily to the disadvantage of those who live there. One example noted by Ligertwood (1984: 205) concerns young people living in the remote Pitjantjatjara communities in the north-west of the State. Before a magistrate can commit a youth to detention, an Assessment Panel must meet and consider the case. Yet because such Panels do not exist in the north-west, children requiring assessment must be remanded to Adelaide to await their sentence. To avoid this compulsory trip to the city for the young offender, the magistrate generally avoids making a detention order, opting instead for an alternative (and lesser) penalty. This may help to explain why so few young Aborigines from the remote areas of the State receive sentences of detention — a situation which could change if assessment and detention facilities became available locally. Conversely, local conditions may produce negative results. Ligertwood (1984: 200) notes that police operating in the Pitjantjatjara lands sometimes choose to arrest a youth on relatively minor matters. This not only removes the offender from the community but it is also seen as punishment in itself, since the youth must find his or her own way back home, a distance of several hundred kilometres. Obviously, such justification for arresting rather than reporting young offenders does not apply in an urban environment.

The impact of police discretion cannot be over-emphasised. Police play a crucial role at various stages of the pre-trial process: apprehension, the decision to arrest or report a youth, and the Screening Panel's determination of the procedural future of a case. Not only can police be expected to exercise discretion differently in different areas for various social reasons, but variations in police numbers may also be relevant. Especially in large urban centres, there is a clear relationship between rates of apprehension and the size of the police force. Areas which experience heavy policing are likely to have high apprehension and arrest rates. Many Aboriginal workers feel that the mere presence of police provokes a reaction from Aboriginal youth which in turn results in their arrest. The role played by the police will be analysed in more detail in subsequent chapters of this book.

Individuals versus Appearances

Like official records elsewhere, the South Australian statistics on youth offending are compiled on the basis of the number of appearances which take place, rather than on the number of individuals who appear. However, a system of cross-classification built into the South Australian computer files makes it possible to determine how many individuals are involved. It can thus be ascertained whether the gross over-representation of Aborigines in the appearance figures is due to a large number of Aborigines being apprehended, or, alternatively, to a relatively small number of young people being apprehended repeatedly.

During the five-year study period, a total of 1424 Aboriginal youths came into contact with the juvenile justice system. More than one-half of these recorded multiple apprehensions. In fact, 58.0 per cent appeared at least twice during this time, while 20.1 per cent made at least five appearances. The average was 3.0 appearances per individual. Official appearance figures therefore over-estimate by some two-thirds the numbers of Aboriginal youths involved.

For non-Aboriginal youth offenders, the discrepancy between appearance-based and individual-based figures is not as great. Of the 26,984 non-Aboriginal youths who entered the juvenile justice system during the five years, almost three-quarters (73.4 per cent) were apprehended only once. Conversely, only just over one-quarter appeared on two or more occasions while a mere 3.6 per cent faced five or more hearings. Overall, white youth averaged 1.5 appearances per individual. As a result, their appearance figures are not as distorted as are those of Aboriginal youth.

Thus it is evident that Aborigines are not as 'criminal' as the appearance figures suggest. Instead, the repeated apprehension of a comparatively small number of Aborigines exaggerates their representation in the official records. This in no way explains why some young Aborigines are selected for such disproportionate attention by police, but it does go some way towards explaining the very large over-representation of Aboriginal youth in the appearance-based crime records.

Yet the method of compiling youth offending statistics according to the number of appearances rather than the number of individuals who appear can offer only a partial explanation for that over-representation. The problem is much more complex than this because, even on an individual basis, Aborigines are noticeably over-represented at the point of entry into the South Australian juvenile justice system.

During the five-year study period, 5.0 per cent of all individuals brought into the system for formal processing were Aboriginal. Yet this group comprised only 1.2 per cent of all youth in the State. On average during each of the five years considered, for every 1000 Aboriginal youth in the population, 132.8 were processed at least once by the juvenile justice system. In contrast, the average annual rate for non-Aboriginal youth was only 30.3 per 1000 youth population. Thus, whichever way the official statistics are kept, whether it be on the basis of appearances or individuals, Aborigines grossly outnumber other members of the population in their contact with the criminal justice system.

Conclusion

In every part of South Australia, Aboriginal youth are subjected to the harsher treatment options at all stages of the criminal process than their non-Aboriginal counterparts. They are substantially more likely to be apprehended and brought into the system than are members of any other ethnic group examined. Once the decision to initiate criminal proceedings has been taken, Aborigines are subsequently more likely to be arrested rather than reported by police; to be referred to the Children's Court rather than diverted to Aid Panels; and, once before the Children's Court, to be sentenced to detention. Not only are they disproportionately involved at each of these stages, but the degree of their disadvantage is compounded as they move through the system, to the extent that, at the final point of sentencing, their chances of being imprisoned are twenty-three times greater than their population size would suggest.

Substantial social and legislative reforms have apparently failed to improve the disadvantaged position of Aboriginal youth before the law. In fact, despite a major restructuring of the juvenile justice legislation in 1971 and in 1979, the position of Aborigines in relation to their non-Aboriginal counterparts has actually deteriorated. It could be argued that each attempt to refine the system by adding to the range of treatment options has had a negative impact on this minority group. When a Court appearance was the only option available, the potential for such extensive differential treatment did not exist. The introduction of Aid Panels in 1972 changed this, by providing a choice of procedural futures for a case.

This 'choice' has consistently resulted in proportionately more Aborigines than non-Aborigines being sent to Court, to their distinct disadvantage. Unless legislative intent can be translated in practice, changes to a system which involve the multiplication of procedural options may, for some groups, produce the opposite effect from that intended.

The wealth of data available in South Australia confirms, from every viewpoint, the enormous degree of difference in the treatment of young Aborigines by the criminal justice system. The rest of the book presents a detailed analysis of the operation of that system, in order to identify the reasons behind this differential treatment.

4
Profile of the Aboriginal Young Offender

The fact that young Aborigines participate in the juvenile justice system in South Australia in vastly disproportionate numbers and that their over-representation varies considerably from one location to another raises important questions. Are they over-represented because they are charged differently from other groups in society? Are their personal, social or locational characteristics so distinct from those of other youths that different treatment may be inevitable? Within the Aboriginal group itself are there regional differences in recorded offending behaviour which may be sufficient to account for the regional differences in treatment?

This chapter demonstrates that Aboriginal young offenders do differ from other young offenders, both in their legal history and their socio-economic circumstances. These differences in the profiles of the two groups offer a potential explanation for the differential treatment of young Aborigines in the criminal justice process. But why such dramatic differences? How much of this is due to either overt or covert racism operating in the criminal justice process?

The Legal Profile

The legal profile of a young offender has three aspects: the crimes with which he or she is charged, the number of charges laid per appearance and the past criminal records. In all three, Aborigines differ from other youth. They are charged with more serious offences; they have more charges laid against them; and they are more likely to have a history of prior appearances before Aid Panels and the Children's Court than non-Aborigines.

Differences in recorded offending behaviour do not necessarily imply differences in real behaviour, since the type and number of charges imposed reflect police discretion. Nevertheless, once a youth enters the formal justice system, behaviour ascribed to that youth by police at the point of contact and officially recorded in police apprehension reports is subsequently deemed to be an accurate portrayal of real behaviour. In effect, recorded data become reality, and these recorded facts are made available to the people involved in decision-making at subsequent stages in the criminal process. Differences between Aboriginal and non-Aboriginal youths in the recorded charge patterns may therefore help to explain why the outcomes recorded for the two groups are different, especially at the level of Screening Panels and Courts.

Types of Offences

According to existing research, adult Aborigines are charged with quite different offences from other adults. After examining the charges against adult Aborigines and whites in Western Australia in 1965, Eggleston (1976: 13) concluded that the 'offences with which Aborigines are charged and of which they are convicted, fall into a distinct pattern which contrasts sharply with the white one'. Almost two decades later, Martin and Newby (1984: 298) reaffirmed this finding. They concluded that

> a pattern of charging for 'petty nuisance' offences — breaches of 'good order' followed by summary arrest — still constitutes the major vehicle whereby Aborigines are introduced into the criminal justice system; whereas whites are most likely to enter via the more regulatory summons-oriented medium of traffic offences.

The South Australian Office of Crime Statistics in 1981 also noted that although Aborigines represented only 2 per cent of that State's rural population, 'more than 5.8 per cent of all [adult] defendants appearing on drunkenness, vagrancy, offensive behaviour and liquor-related charges' in country Courts were Aboriginal (Courts of Summary Jurisdiction, 1 January–30 June 1981: 20).

The predominance of alcohol-related 'petty nuisance' offences among adults has, through persistent media coverage, come to be regarded by white Australians as almost a normal feature of Aboriginal life and a major contributor to their over-involvement in the criminal justice system. By contrast, although few researchers have investigated the patterns of recorded juvenile crime, the general indication is that such charges do not characterise young Aboriginal offenders. Instead, amongst juveniles, there is far greater emphasis on property offences, such as break and enter, larceny and vehicle theft. These offences accounted for some 71 per cent of all Aboriginal youth convictions on Groote Eylandt in 1974–75 (Gilroy, 1976), 50 per cent of all juvenile cases handled by the Aboriginal and Torres Strait Islander Legal Service in Queensland in 1980 (Foley,

1982) 86 per cent of all charges laid against Aboriginal youths in Bourke in 1982 (Chisholm, 1983) and 77 per cent of all offences cited against Aboriginal juveniles in North-West New South Wales in the year ending 30 June 1986 (Cunneen and Robb, 1987: 142). Similarly, 74 per cent of all male Aboriginal youths held in corrective institutions in New South Wales in July 1982 were there because of various forms of theft.

An analysis of the major charges[1] laid against all Aboriginal and non-Aboriginal youth appearing in South Australia over the five-year study

Table 4.1: Major charge: comparison between Aboriginal and non-Aboriginal appearances

Major charge	Aborigines %	Non-Aborigines %
Assault occasioning bodily harm	0.8	0.5
Common assault	6.9	3.9
Robbery with violence	0.9	0.4
Total offences against person	8.6	4.8
Break, enter, steal	28.4	12.5
Break, enter with intent	3.3	1.3
Illegal use, interference to a motor vehicle	14.7	5.8
Larceny	10.7	16.2
Shoplifting	4.0	23.0
Total offences against property	61.1	58.8
Assault, hinder police	0.9	0.6
Disorderly, offensive behaviour	6.5	4.3
Drunk in public place*	3.6	1.0
Unlawfully on premises	1.5	1.5
Loitering	0.9	0.7
Total offences against good order	13.4	8.1
Motor vehicle, road traffic violations	1.2	3.9
Wilful damage	4.3	3.8
Receiving	2.6	1.9
Unlawful possession	0.4	0.6
False pretences, embezzlement	0.3	1.9
Minor consuming, obtaining liquor	1.8	2.2
Use or possess drugs	0.5	3.2
Carry offensive weapon use firearm to annoy, endanger no firearm licence	0.7	2.5
Other	5.1	8.3
TOTAL	100.0 n=3310	100.0 n=39193

*This offence was decriminalised in 1984.

period supports these findings. Table 4.1 shows that in South Australia offences against property represent by far the most common charges laid against both Aboriginal and non-Aboriginal youth alike, featuring in well over one-half of all youth appearances. The proportions for each group are fairly similar: 61.1 per cent of all Aboriginal appearances and 58.8 per cent of all non-Aboriginal appearances. In this State, as elsewhere in Australia, theft is thus the predominant juvenile offence, and in this there are no obvious inter-group differences. Yet important variations between Aboriginal and non-Aboriginal youth do emerge when specific offences within this category are examined, with young Aborigines more likely to be charged with serious property offences. In particular, the offence of break, enter, steal accounts for the highest proportion of all Aboriginal appearances, whereas the relatively trivial offence of shoplifting accounts for the greatest proportion of non-Aboriginal appearances. A similar pattern emerges for illegal vehicle use and larceny. A far greater percentage of Aboriginal than non-Aboriginal appearances involve the relatively serious offence of illegal use of or interference to a motor vehicle. The converse is true for the less serious crime of larceny.

Since the charges recorded against a youth may not necessarily reflect actual offending behaviour, it is not clear to what extent Aborigines actually commit more serious property offences or whether other factors and, in particular, police discretion in charging, are at work. At the point of apprehension, a police officer must select, from a range of possible charges, that which in his or her estimation most appropriately reflects the illegal behaviour observed. For example, a youth who opens the door and enters an unlocked garage on a person's property and steals an item of minor value may be charged with breaking and entering. Alternatively, he or she could be charged with being unlawfully on premises or larceny. Nor does police discretion end here. At the pre-trial stage, the police prosecutor, usually as a result of negotiations with the youth's lawyer, may agree to drop the original charges, and substitute new ones. In one case observed, a youth was charged by the apprehending officers with the single count of robbery with violence. Before the matter came to trial, charges of larceny from the person and assault were substituted, and were subsequently listed in the official records.

Even if young Aborigines do commit more serious offences, this may not reflect greater 'criminality' but different environmental opportunities and pressures. To illustrate, shoplifting, commonly regarded as a minor property offence, is an urban crime clearly related to the presence of department stores and supermarkets. Yet many Aboriginal property offences take place in remote communities where it would be difficult to classify any form of theft, no matter how trivial, as shoplifting. Any attempt to steal from a store in an outback area will almost inevitably lead to charges of larceny or break and enter. It is no coincidence that during the five-year study period, only two young Aborigines living in the remote areas of South Australia were charged with shoplifting, compared with ninety Adelaide-based Aborigines. Inevitably then, non-Aborigines who live almost entirely in large urban centres have a greater opportunity to shoplift simply because of their residential location. Yet even in a city such as Adelaide, it could be argued that environmental factors still dissuade Aborigines from shoplifting. As one young Aboriginal explained, she and her friends 'stood out a mile' whenever they entered a large department store and were aware of being closely watched by the store's security personnel. Any temptation to shoplift is countered by the high probability of detection. Non-Aboriginal youths are less noticeable, and so believe that they have a reasonable chance of 'getting away' with this offence. It is therefore not only a matter of real opportunity to offend but also of perceived opportunity.

The frequency with which young Aborigines are charged with illegal use of or interference to a motor vehicle may also be partly explained by location. In small rural or remote communities where isolation is predominant, young people tend to 'borrow' vehicles, often from white staff of the community, to enable them to achieve mobility and temporary escape from their limited environment. Brady and Morice (1982: 92) relate one incident when a group of thirteen stole a utility from the remote West Coast settlement of Yalata and, by transferring in turn to several other stolen vehicles after their original one ran out of petrol, they finally reached Indulkana, a Pitjantjatjara community 500 kilometres to the north of Yalata. Young people in the city have different opportunities for mobility. Also relevant is the different extent to which Aboriginal and non-Aboriginal youth have legitimate access to vehicles. Because of the much higher rate of car ownership amongst the white population, non-Aboriginal youth are more likely to have access to a car belonging to a friend or a member of the family. The significance of this is highlighted by a recent incident in Adelaide, where State Transport Authority officials refused to allow a group of young Aborigines to board the last train leaving the city for the northern satellite district of Elizabeth. It was almost midnight, they had no money to hire a taxi, they were unable to contact their parents who were not on the telephone and they knew of no-one who had access to a car and could pick them up. To solve this 'crisis', they stole a car to transport them home. In this case, the motive for the offence was the result of the actions of the State Transport Authority officials. The subsequent apprehension of this group by police was virtually inevitable, since a car overcrowded with young blacks in the early hours of the morning is highly visible. Nor does the relatively large number of 'illegal use' charges laid against young Aborigines necessarily mean that all are guilty of actual car theft. We have documented numerous instances where one or possibly two youths steal the vehicle and then proceed to pick up and give lifts to other young Aborigines walking along the street or waiting at bus stops. As a result, when finally stopped by police, there may be six or seven people in the car. Some, if not most, of them do not realise they are in a stolen vehicle. Yet all are charged with 'illegal use'.

Offences against good order, more commonly referred to as 'street' offences since they occur predominantly in public places, represent the second most common set of charges laid against both Aboriginal and non-Aboriginal youth. Of all the charges laid, it is these which generate the most resentment within the Aboriginal community and form the basis for claims that police discriminate against them. Numerous stories circulate about Aborigines being arrested and charged with disorderly behaviour while 'just walking down the street'. There is a tendency for those who consider themselves singled out for unjust treatment by police to retaliate with abusive behaviour, which can rapidly escalate to a physical confrontation and subsequent charges of assaulting and hindering police. The fact that a higher proportion of Aboriginal than non-Aboriginal appearances (13.4 per cent compared with 8.1 per cent) involved a street offence as the major charge may provide some support for this claim of police discrimination. Yet in view of the frequency with which reports of such incidents circulated within the Aboriginal community, the figures are lower than expected. One explanation may be that, whilst Aborigines are originally stopped and questioned by police for a street offence, they may subsequently be charged with different offences. Observation in popular street locations indicated that the presence of large and often noisy groups of Aboriginal youth initially attracted police intervention. The police then carried out on-the-spot checks for outstanding warrants which not infrequently led to the arrest of some of them for prior offences, many of which were theft-related. It is also possible that the general perceptions of the Aboriginal community regarding the predominance of street offences may be inaccurate. In discussions with Aboriginal parents, lawyers and even police, the issue of interaction between police and Aborigines in the public domain aroused the greatest concern and comment. Such interaction is highly visible, simply because it takes place in crowded, public arenas, with many casual on-lookers. In addition, it often results in physical confrontation which adds to its visibility. Aboriginal and police awareness of such incidents is therefore extremely high, perhaps giving rise to an over-estimation of their importance in the overall offending profile of young Aborigines.

Crimes against the person, generally regarded as extremely serious offences, are not commonly laid against juveniles. Nevertheless, such offences were listed as the major charge in almost double the proportion of Aboriginal as non-Aboriginal cases. This is principally due to the larger proportion of common assault charges brought against Aboriginal youth. These differences might support the positivist argument that poor living conditions lead to a greater degree of violence in Aboriginal communities. Yet it may reflect nothing more than the well-documented fact that violence in an Aboriginal community is often an open and public event to which police are readily called. In contrast, the occurrence of domestic conflict in a non-Aboriginal suburban home may not be reported and even if it is, the reluctance of police to proceed with assault charges in this context is well known.

The remaining offences recorded in Table 4.1 account for a relatively small proportion of total appearances and in general the differences between the two groups are quite minor. Nevertheless, some interesting points do emerge. The so-called 'white-collar' crimes of false pretences and embezzlement are more commonly cited as the major charge in non-Aboriginal than in Aboriginal appearances. The same applies for the offence of using or possessing drugs, and violations against the Motor Vehicle and Road Traffic Acts.

Clearly then, Aboriginal and non-Aboriginal youth differ in the types of offence charges laid against them. There is some evidence that young Aborigines are more likely than their non-Aboriginal counterparts to be charged with more serious offences, and in particular, offences against the person and serious offences against property. This is not to say that the actual offending behaviour of these two groups is different: merely, that the recorded charge patterns are not the same. The main difference in the charge profiles rests in the distinction between different types of property offences. In fact, of the 165 possible charges, two offences only accounted for 43.1 per cent of all Aboriginal appearances; these two being the more serious property offences of break, enter and steal, and illegal use of or interference to a motor vehicle. Similarly, two offences only accounted for 39.2 per cent of all appearances by non-Aboriginal youth, but these were the less serious property charges of shoplifting and larceny. As already pointed out, these differences may be more a product of locational opportunities and pressures than of criminal preferences. Nevertheless, these dissimilarities may be sufficient to account for the variation in outcomes recorded for Aboriginal and non-Aboriginal youth at subsequent stages of the criminal process.

Number of Offences

When apprehended, Aboriginal youth are not only charged with somewhat more serious offences than their non-Aboriginal counterparts, but they also have a significantly larger number of charges laid against them. Almost one-half (46.2 per cent) of all Aboriginal cases involved more than one charge compared with only 27.3 per cent of the non-Aboriginal cases. Moreover, a higher proportion of Aboriginal than non-Aboriginal appearances involved four or more offence charges: 9.9 per cent compared with 3.8 per cent.

Although comparative data from other areas of Australia are extremely scarce, there is some indication that these findings are not unique to South Australia. Our result for Aboriginal youth is very similar to that obtained by Chisholm (1983: 20). His study in Nowra, New South Wales, revealed that some 44.8 per cent of all Aboriginal appearances before the Children's Court during the first half of 1982 involved multiple charges, with a mean of 2.7 charges per child. Eggleston (1976) found evidence of the more frequent use of multiple charging amongst Aboriginal compared with non-Aboriginal adults yet, compared with the figures on South Australian juveniles, hers were relatively low. She recorded multiple charges in only 17.4 per cent of all Aboriginal appearances compared with an even lower figure of 12.9 per cent for whites.

Whilst Aborigines may commit more offences at a given time than non-Aborigines, aspects of the criminal justice process itself may once again contribute to this pattern of difference. For instance, it has been suggested that with the increasing availability of legal representation through the Aboriginal Legal Rights Movement, police now deliberately lay more charges against Aboriginal youths at the point of apprehension, to compensate for the possibility that some of these will be dropped during pre-trial negotiations. Another factor may be the group nature of Aboriginal offending. Although not recorded in official statistics, it is widely recognised that young Aborigines frequently act in groups. Since each individual in the group may subsequently be charged with the combined offences of the entire group, the number of counts per person may be extremely high. This will inevitably inflate the charge statistics. Illegal use of a motor vehicle almost always involves a group rather than individual Aborigines, and such groups tend to be large, with six, eight or even ten youths acting in consort. On one occasion, for example, two youths stole a car from an Adelaide car park, and drove along Hindley Street where they picked up three friends. They then visited a house in a nearby suburb, where two more youths joined them. A short time later, the vehicle ran out of petrol, and all seven were apprehended by police as they tried to leave the car. They were variously charged with illegal use, driving without a licence, driving without due care, resisting arrest and assaulting police.

Other researchers recount similar examples. Brady and Morice (1982), for example, relate details of an incident of vehicle theft at Yalata involving thirteen adolescents. In another incident, eight boys broke into a house on the reserve and stole some money. At the same time, they also found the keys to the home owner's car, which they proceeded to steal and drive to another Aboriginal community some 1000 kilometres away. On the way, they stole petrol and food. The original criminal act thus led to a string of subsequent, essentially opportunistic offences, all of which were ultimately laid against each of the youths involved.

Prior Offending Records

Dramatic differences between Aboriginal and non-Aboriginal youth were also apparent in terms of their prior contact with the system. Young Aborigines drawn into formal contact with the justice system were significantly more likely to have a record of previous appearances before both Aid Panels and the Children's Court. In addition, they were more likely to be the subject of an existing order at the time of their apprehension.

Table 4.2 details the number of previous Aid Panel appearances accumulated by young people during the five-year period under consideration. As shown, the majority of appearances by non-Aborigines involved young people who had not previously come before an Aid Panel. In contrast, less than one-half of Aboriginal appearances involved youth

Table 4.2: Prior Aid Panel and Court appearance records of Aboriginal and non-Aboriginal youth

Number of previous appearances	Number of previous Aid Panel appearances		Number of previous Children's Court appearances	
	Aborigines %	Non-Aborigines %	Aborigines %	Non-Aborigines %
0	42.9	67.9	39.6	74.0
1	25.5	18.4	16.8	12.1
2	16.1	8.4	11.3	5.3
3 or more	15.5	5.3	32.3	8.6
Total	100.0	100.0	100.0	100.0
	n=3310	n=39193	n=3310	n=39193

without a prior Aid Panel record. At the other end of the scale, the proportion of Aboriginal appearances involving youth with three or more previous Aid Panel appearances was almost three times greater than the corresponding figure recorded for non-Aborigines.

Even larger differences between the two groups were evident in relation to the number of previous Children's Court appearances. Table 4.2 illustrates that almost three-quarters of all non-Aboriginal appearances involved persons who had not previously come before the Children's Court. The same situation applied in considerably less than half of the Aboriginal appearances. Moreover, only a very small proportion of non-Aboriginal appearances recorded three or more previous Court hearings, compared with almost one-third of the Aboriginal appearances.

This finding that the same Aborigines are apprehended much more frequently by police than are non-Aborigines may indicate that young Aborigines re-offend more often than their white counterparts. However, an equally credible explanation may be found in the momentum of official notice: once an Aboriginal youth (highly visible in the first place) has come into formal contact with the system, the chances of avoiding future processing are extremely low. In short, the process may be self-generating. Interviews conducted with young Aborigines revealed that many of those who had long criminal records perceived themselves to be 'picked on' by police, not only because of their visibility in a predominantly 'white' environment but also because they belonged to families which had a reputation for getting into trouble. It was not unusual for a young person with an offending record to come from a household where other family members had spent time in prison. Such young people felt that they were continually being harassed and charged simply because they and their families were well known to police and were relatively easy 'targets'.

Final evidence that Aborigines experience greater contact with the system is derived from an analysis of those appearances which took place while the youth was either an absconder or still the subject of an order imposed during an earlier hearing (such as bail or supervision).[2] This situation applied in almost one-quarter (24.6 per cent) of all Aboriginal cases, compared with a mere 7.2 per cent of all non-Aboriginal cases. Two types of orders, namely supervision orders and bail orders, were responsible for most of this difference. These accounted for 19.4 per cent and 4.6 per cent of all Aboriginal appearances respectively, but only 5.4 per cent and 1.2 per cent of all non-Aboriginal appearances. The proportion of appearances involving absconders was extremely small for both groups; namely, 0.3 per cent of Aboriginal cases compared with 0.1 per cent of non-Aboriginal cases.

On the basis of these three factors — prior Aid Panel records, prior Court records and existing Court orders — it is obvious that Aboriginal youth exhibit a greater degree of contact with the juvenile justice system than do non-Aboriginal youth. Thus, not only are Aborigines over-represented in terms of the numbers who are initially apprehended and who are taken into the juvenile justice system, but once in the system, they experience more contact with it than other young offenders.

Geographical Variations in the Legal Profile of Young Aborigines

So far, this sketch of the young Aboriginal's legal profile has been drawn from overall appearances throughout the State. Yet Chapter 3 detailed dramatic geographical variations in the degree of Aboriginal over-representation in the system. Can these be explained by geographical variations in the legal profile itself?

It is self-evident that Aboriginal youth living within the remote, traditionally oriented communities of the Far North and North West of the State pursue quite different lifestyles, with different values, expectations and opportunities from Aboriginal youth living in southern communities such as Point Pearce and Point McLeay or those integrated within white rural towns. In turn, the lifestyle of rural youth would differ from those of young Aborigines living in the metropolitan area of Adelaide.

In fact, it was Aboriginal recognition of these different lifestyles and opportunities which prompted the large-scale migration of many Aboriginal families to the urban centres (and particularly to Adelaide) during the 1950s and 1960s. They saw the city as a place where they could be free of the restrictive environment of the reserve and where their children would benefit from greater access to education, housing and medical care. They also perceived the city to be a socially more advantageous environment than the rural communities in which they themselves had been reared. A study of Aborigines in Adelaide in 1966 (Gale, 1972) supported this view. It showed that the crime rates of Aboriginal youth in Adelaide were substantially lower than those of young Aborigines on reserves. Yet this now seems to have been a temporary situation resulting from particular historic events. As indicated in Chapter 3, there is now clear evidence that

Aboriginal youth in many rural areas and particularly in the remote North West of the State are less likely to get into trouble with police than those in the city. Even when apprehension does occur, Aboriginal youth in these remote areas are less likely to be arrested, sent to Court and ultimately detained than are their Aboriginal counterparts in Adelaide. In contrast with a decade ago, Aboriginal mothers living in Adelaide now indicate that young people need to be sent back to the country to 'keep them out of trouble'. As a result, the ever-increasing stream of urban migrants of the 1950s and 1960s has largely ceased. However, not all rural-based young people are 'better off' than the city dwellers. Treatment for young Aborigines living in the Point Pearce Aboriginal community located on the Yorke Peninsula, for example, still seems to be abnormally harsh.

Given the differences in lifestyles and opportunities, it is possible that the nature of offending amongst Aboriginal youth would vary according to location. If this were the case, then such regional differences should be recorded in the official statistics. However, the data are not wholly consistent with this hypothesis. Although some regional variations in the charge profile are evident, these are relatively slight and nowhere near substantial enough to account for the very marked regional differences which exist in the degree of Aboriginal over-representation at each point in the juvenile justice process. To understand this it is simplest to divide the State into three locations, namely the capital city of Adelaide, the remote West and North West, and the remaining rural areas of the State. In all three broadly defined areas, offences against property predominated. These formed the major charge in some 58.5 per cent of all appearances by Adelaide youth, 62.5 per cent of appearances by rural youth and 63.3 per cent of appearances by those living in the remote region of South Australia. There were, however, variations within this general offence grouping. A higher proportion of remote-based youth (39.2 per cent) were charged with break and enter than was the case for rural-based Aborigines (31.3 per cent) or Adelaide youth (21.6 per cent). Conversely, there was a slightly higher proportion of larceny charges amongst Adelaide residents (11.9 per cent) compared with those living in remote South Australia (8.0 per cent). As expected, almost all shoplifting charges laid against Aboriginal youth involved Adelaide residents.

In relation to all other charges, differences between the three areas were small, and in some cases, surprisingly so. For example, there were no appreciable regional variations in the proportion of youth charged with 'street' offences, despite heavy policing in central Adelaide, where clashes with Aborigines are common. In fact, the proportion of Adelaide youth charged with offences against public order was almost the same as the proportion of those from remote areas: 14.9 per cent compared with 16.0 per cent.

Table 4.3 highlights the similarity in charge profiles for the three regions by ranking offences in order of frequency. In all three geographical areas, break enter steal, illegal use of or interference to a motor vehicle and larceny are ranked in first, second and third positions.

Table 4.3: A regional comparison of the six major charges most frequently imposed on Aboriginal youth

Rank	Adelaide		Rural S.A.		Remote S.A.	
	Major charge	% of total appearances	Major charge	% of total appearances	Major charge	% of total appearances
1	Break, enter, steal	21.6	Break, enter, steal	31.3	Break, enter, steal	39.2
2	Vehicle theft	15.2	Vehicle theft	14.6	Vehicle theft	13.0
3	Larceny	11.9	Larceny	10.2	Larceny	8.0
4	Common assault	7.2	Common assault	7.0	Disorderly behaviour	6.8
5	Disorderly behaviour	7.2	Disorderly behaviour	6.0	Common assault	5.6
6	Shoplifting	6.9	Wilful damage	5.1	Wilful damage	5.6

Common assault and disorderly behaviour occupy the next two ranks, although the ordering in the remote area varies from that recorded for the other two regions. It is only in relation to the sixth-ranked offence that real differences emerge. Shoplifting occupies this position in Adelaide but is displaced in rural and remote areas by wilful damage. On the basis of these results, it could be argued that differences in the charges laid are insufficient to account for the regional variations in Aboriginal apprehensions, arrests, Court appearances and detention rates observed earlier.

The number of offence charges laid at any one time varied even less than the major charge from one area to another and thus could contribute little to an explanation of the marked differences in regional rates of apprehension or treatment. This was true, even when comparing remote South Australia with metropolitan Adelaide. During the five-year study period, Aboriginal youth living in the Far North and North West of the State were only slightly less likely to be charged with multiple offences than were their Adelaide counterparts (41.0 per cent compared with 47.1 per cent).

However, the past criminal record of offenders presented a very different picture. Here regional differences were marked. More specifically, young Aborigines from the remote areas of South Australia experienced the least amount of previous contact, while young people from Adelaide recorded the most contact. The majority of appearances in remote South Australia involved Aborigines with no prior Aid Panel record (61.4 per cent) and no previous Court record (56.5 per cent). This contrasts strongly with the situation in Adelaide, where only 36.8 per cent of all Aboriginal appearances involved a young man or woman who had no previous Aid Panel record while 35.7 per cent had no prior Court record. The situation for rural-based Aborigines more closely resembled that of their Adelaide counterparts than that of the remote dwellers. Some 42.8 per cent and 39.0 per cent of appearances by such youth involved no previous Aid Panel or Court appearance respectively. Similar contrasts were evident when looking at appearances by young Aborigines who were under an existing Court order. This applied to well over one-quarter (29.3 per cent) of all appearances by Adelaide-based Aboriginal youth. The corresponding figure for rural areas was somewhat lower (24.3 per cent), while that for the remote region was lower still (10.5 per cent).

Thus in terms of prior records, there are clear regional differences in the offending profiles of young Aborigines. In particular, fewer young people in remote areas have records of prior contact with the system than is the case in Adelaide. This may help to explain the milder treatment accorded them during judicial processing. However, with respect to the other legal variables, evidence which may justify milder treatment for remote youth is both insufficient and contradictory. Our findings showed the Aborigines from remote areas were only slightly less likely to have multiple charges laid against them than their city counterparts. The nature of the offence charges were also generally similar in all three regions. The small variations which did exist did not accord with treatment patterns. Remote Aborigines were more likely than their Adelaide counterparts to be charged with the more serious property offences (namely: break, enter, steal), while the minor charge of shoplifting was more prevalent, as expected, in the city. In effect then, youth from remote areas were charged more frequently than city youth with offences which usually merit harsher treatment. This completely contradicts the finding of 'milder' treatment for the remote dwellers and raises numerous questions concerning the different charge patterns from one place to another. Generally speaking, all that can be said here is that regional variations in the legal profile of the Aboriginal young offender are not sufficiently marked to furnish even the beginnings of an adequate explanation for the dramatic regional differences in the treatment of Aborigines by the juvenile justice system.

The Socio-economic Profile

Earlier in this chapter, attention was drawn to the fact that in most areas of Australia empirical data on the nature and frequency of offending by Aboriginal youth are non-existent. Even less information is available on the personal characteristics of these young offenders. Nevertheless, personal and socio-economic characteristics may assume great importance in the juvenile justice system because of its emphasis on individualised treatment.

in illegal activities is essentially a male prerogative, and South Australian youth, both Aboriginal and white, proved to be no exception. The overwhelming majority (78.1 per cent) of those appearances which took place during the five-year study period involved males and this applied irrespective of whether they were Aboriginal or not. Male involvement in the South Australian juvenile justice system was only slightly more pronounced amongst Aboriginal than non-Aboriginal youth, accounting for 81.4 per cent of the Aboriginal appearances compared with 77.9 per cent of the non-Aboriginal appearances. This finding illustrates that this book is dealing primarily with recorded male crime.

Nor were there major differences in age structure, although as was the case in North-West New South Wales (Cunneen and Robb, 1987: 141), a slightly greater proportion of Aboriginal than non-Aboriginal appearances involved young children aged twelve years and under; namely, 15.2 per cent compared with 11.6 per cent respectively. Conversely, at the other end of the scale, seventeen-year-olds accounted for a slightly greater proportion of non-Aboriginal than Aboriginal appearances (20.4 per cent compared with 18.1 per cent). Thus Aborigines appearing before the Children's Court or Aid Panels are only slightly younger and slightly more likely to be male than their non-Aboriginal counterparts.

Interviews conducted amongst Aboriginal households in Adelaide (Gale and Wundersitz, 1982) revealed living standards which were generally well below those of mainstream society. Extremely high unemployment levels, especially amongst males, resulted in low incomes and heavy reliance on social security payments. Patterns of house occupancy and family structure also differed from those which characterised the general community, even in the same residential areas. Aboriginal households generally consisted of multi-family units controlled by single females, and an overwhelming reliance on rental accommodation. These differences in social background are reflected in the young people entering the juvenile justice system.

At the time of their apprehension a large proportion of young offenders were still at school. This applied to 64.8 per cent of all non-Aboriginal cases and 53.9 per cent of all Aboriginal cases. However, if analysis is limited to school-leavers only (that is, to those technically in the workforce), two dramatic findings emerge. Firstly, there are extremely high levels of unemployment in both groups. Secondly, within this framework of high unemployment, the unemployment rate of young Aboriginal offenders far exceeded that of their white counterparts. In fact, 91.2 per cent of appearances by Aboriginal school-leavers involved those who were unemployed. The corresponding figure for white youth, namely 61.4 per cent, was still high, but not as extreme as the Aboriginal situation.

This extraordinarily high unemployment rate amongst apprehended Aboriginal youth mirrors the high unemployment rates amongst young people in the wider Aboriginal community. The Adelaide household survey (Gale and Wundersitz, 1982) found that, amongst those individuals aged 15–19 years technically in the workforce, some 79.4 per cent were unemployed and only 20.6 per cent were employed. Unemployment levels in rural and remote areas of the State, where the majority of Aborigines live, is even higher than in the city. If there is a close association between unemployment and the likelihood of apprehension, the disadvantages accruing to Aboriginal youths from this employment pattern may be substantial.

Differences in household structure between Aboriginal and non-Aboriginal young offenders are also very pronounced. Whereas 63.5 per cent of non-Aboriginal appearances involved young people who lived within a 'normative' nuclear family headed by his or her two natural parents, the same applied to only 28.3 per cent of Aboriginal appearances. By contrast, the majority of Aboriginal appearances were by persons who lived in single-parent families or with foster parents or relatives. The former category accounted for 35.5 per cent of all Aboriginal appearances while the latter accounted for one-quarter. Corresponding figures for the non-Aboriginal group were considerably lower. Children from single-parent families accounted for 23.5 per cent of appearances, while those living in foster homes or with relatives featured in a mere 3.7 per cent. The high level of fostering among Aboriginal offenders reflects the situation in the broader Aboriginal community. For many years, the State Government actively pursued a policy of removing children from their parents and placing them in white institutions or with white families. This policy was based on the belief that separating such children from Aboriginal influences would facilitate the process of assimilation, especially in the case of part-Aborigines born to tribal women. Although the extent of this removal has never been accurately documented, a 1966 survey of Aborigines in Adelaide (Gale, 1972) found that of the 2039 individuals resident in the city, approximately 13 per cent were children brought there 'by government or voluntary agencies for placement in a foster home . . . or . . . children's institution' (p. 87). This policy has now been changed, largely as a result of pressures from the Aboriginal community who saw the benefits of Aboriginal children being placed in the home of a relative. In fact, in 1988 the *Children's Protection and Young Offenders Act* was amended to include in section 7 the factor of 'the child's ethnic or racial background and the need to guard against damage to the child's sense of cultural identity'. However, this development post-dates by many years the young people who are described in this book. For them, the process of being fostered in white homes, where they were often denied any contact with their own community, meant that they became well-known to both welfare agencies and the police. In fact, it was the police who often performed the task of physically removing the child from his or her family. From this point on the child became the subject of close scrutiny from authority figures. This in turn increased the likelihood that any deviant behaviour would be reported and acted upon.

The relatively small proportion of Aboriginal young offenders who belonged to a nuclear family headed by both parents also reflects the situation within the broader Aboriginal community. The 1982 household survey revealed that, even within the urbanised Aboriginal community in Adelaide, less than one-half of families with children were headed by a couple. Moreover, in many of these instances, either one or both of the adult family heads were not the natural parents of the children.

It is highly likely that such major differences in both household structure and employment status will adversely affect Aboriginal youth who are brought before the juvenile justice system. A model based on welfare and rehabilitation emphasises the personal circumstances and perceived needs of the individual. Section 7 of the *Children's Protection and Young Offenders Act* 1979 (S.A.) (as amended in 1988) requires any Court, Panel or other body or person involved in the Act's administration to exercise their powers 'to secure for the child such care, protection, control, correction or guidance as will best lead to the proper development of his personality and to his development into a responsible and useful member of the community'. Under such a model, there may be a temptation to regard those from low socio-economic groups and non-nuclear families as being deprived and therefore in more need of 'help'. Such help, it is argued, is best provided through interventionist strategies. In line with this, police officers have admitted that they often arrest Aborigines, especially the younger ones, 'for their own good' and 'to get them off the streets'. Although the current South Australian legislation represents a partial retreat from the earlier welfare-dominated model of juvenile justice, and rejects the notion that the commission of a crime should *per se* be the peg on which social welfare intervention is hung, nevertheless other provisions within section 7 are of particular interest in this context. Section 7(b) directs attention to 'the desirability of leaving the child within his [*sic*] own home', and section 7(c) to 'the desirability of allowing the education or employment of the child to continue without interruption'. These ideal objectives may have negative repercussions for young Aborigines who predominantly are without employment and frequently do not reside in a conventional nuclear household. In such cases, if a child is not at school, is unemployed and comes from a single-parent household (which is typically defined as a 'broken' home) then this requirement has no application. Such a child may thus be sent to Court and be sentenced to detention, all on the grounds that it is for his or her 'own good'.

Differences in Residential Location

Variations in the address of Aboriginal and non-Aboriginal youth at the time of their apprehension provide an indirect indication of other types of differences between the two groups for which direct measurements do not exist on the youth-offending data files. Different residential locations reflect differences in socio-economic status, different offending opportunities and even differences in such factors as police strength, Screening Panel procedures and whether a Children's Court appearance is presided over by a magistrate or judge. These in turn substantially affect both the extent and nature of a young person's contact with the justice system.

Aboriginal and non-Aboriginal young offenders have vastly different locational patterns. The former are predominantly rural-based while the latter are, in the main, urban dwellers. Whereas 78.6 per cent of non-Aboriginal appearances involved youth resident in Adelaide at the time of their apprehension, only 40.3 per cent of Aboriginal appearances were by city-based youth. Conversely, 59.7 per cent of Aboriginal appearances were by youth living in rural South Australia or in the remote Far North and North West of the State. Yet, in combination, these rural and remote areas accounted for only a relatively small 21.4 per cent of all non-Aboriginal appearances.

Differences in the residential location of young offenders are also evident within Adelaide itself, with Aborigines tending to live in those suburbs where apprehension rates for all youth were generally high. There is considerable variation in average apprehension rates from one local government area to another in the city, irrespective of race or ethnicity, and in broad terms these seem to be associated with the socio-economic status of the various suburbs. Adelaide is a city with extreme residential stratification based on socio-economic criteria, and in common with other geographic analyses of crime (e.g. Baldwin and Bottoms, 1976; Harries, 1980; Herbert, 1982; Pyle, 1974) it shows a disproportionate spatial distribution of youth apprehensions which can be correlated with the social status of a suburb. The highest apprehension rates are to be found, as expected, in the newer outer housing estates and the older western industrial suburbs close to the city. Thus Elizabeth, a post-war housing trust estate, recorded an annual rate of apprehension for all young people of 94.5 per 1000 of the total population aged 10–17 years inclusive. Thebarton, an older inner industrial area, recorded 88.7 appearances per 1000 youth and Port Adelaide, an old industrial area containing the city's harbour facilities, recorded a rate of 85.3 apprehensions per 1000 youth. By contrast, the higher status suburbs of Walkerville, Stirling and Burnside recorded rates of 20.3, 21.0 and 22.2 per 1000 youth respectively. Not unexpectedly, a greater proportion of Aboriginal than non-Aboriginal young offenders live in those areas where apprehension rates are generally high.

Even within Adelaide then, important locational differences persist between the two racial groups which, in combination with the large urban–rural differences, may help to explain, if not to excuse, the disproportionate number of Aboriginal apprehensions and their subsequent different treatment.

Conclusion

It is all too evident that, on a per capita basis, Aboriginal youth far outnumber others in the degree and frequency of their contact with police and the justice system. It is also evident that Aborigines differ from non-Aborigines in terms of their legal, social and economic profile. Young Aborigines are generally charged with more serious offences; they are subject to a greater number of charges and have longer criminal records. They are more likely than non-Aborigines to be unemployed, to belong to non-nuclear families and to reside either in rural areas or in the lower socio-economic suburbs in the city.

These findings raise a crucial question: are Aborigines over-represented before the criminal justice system because of the operation of overt racism, or is it due to their more serious offending records and/or their low socio-economic status?

Poverty seems to be an inevitable correlate of police notice, with high apprehension rates the world over coinciding with poor economic conditions. Consequently, it may be expected that Aborigines will be substantially over-represented at the point of entry into the juvenile justice system. However, because of the underlying philosophy of that system, such factors may continue to influence decision-making at all subsequent levels. To a far greater degree than its adult counterpart, the juvenile justice system focuses on the individual and the best means of achieving his or her rehabilitation. This philosophy of individualised treatment allows for legitimate consideration to be given to personal and socio-economic characteristics at all points in the system. It is therefore possible that the depressed living conditions of Aborigines are used to justify their harsher treatment not only at the point of apprehension, but also at the levels of Screening Panel referral and Court sentences.

At the same time, however, the legislation makes it clear that legal factors are not to be ignored. Although it does not advocate that the punishment should fit the crime, nevertheless it does emphasise the dual need to protect the community from the criminal behaviour of young people and to ensure that the individual offender be held responsible for his or her behaviour. By so doing, it legitimates any action which gives independent weighting to the seriousness of the offence and existing evidence of prior offending. On this basis, differences between Aboriginal and non-Aboriginal youth in recorded offending behaviour may help to explain why the two groups receive apparently different outcomes, especially at the Screening Panel and Court levels.

The remainder of the book investigates the role played by these various factors in the juvenile justice system in order to determine whether racial discrimination is operative or whether alternative explanations, couched in terms of the legal and socio-economic profile of the young offenders, are more appropriate. Each level of that system will be examined separately: the method of apprehension by police, the decision to divert or send to Court, and the outcome of both Aid Panel and Court appearances. It is crucial to examine each of these stages, since to concentrate solely on the ultimate stage of sentencing creates a distorted picture. It fails to recognise the cost to individuals of their involvement with the process itself, irrespective of its final outcome. It also ignores the fact that the decisions taken early in the criminal justice process may be the crucial ones, since these determine whether or not an accused youth will be diverted out of the system at the pre-Court stage or will face the full weight of a Court hearing.

5

Police: The Initiators of Justice?

Police exert tremendous power at the gateway to all criminal justice systems: they determine who enters and how. It is therefore not surprising that the disproportionate rate of apprehension amongst Aborigines is often cited as evidence of police discrimination. Yet in Australia, little empirical research has as yet been conducted on the specific question of racial bias in the exercise of police discretion. Although the issue of poor relations between Aborigines and police has often been raised, no studies have attempted to assess systematically police behaviour at the point of apprehension. Under what circumstances do police apprehend Aborigines? What determines the nature and number of charges laid, and why do they choose to arrest rather than report so many Aborigines?

The lack of research in this area is of major concern, since arguably, the most crucial decision taken in the whole criminal justice system is the decision that an individual should enter it. Once a person is brought within the formal process, the real costs can be considerable, even if the final outcome entails no conviction or sentence. The police take a decision at the point of apprehension which sets in motion a mechanism which may be slow and frustrating, and which may have a considerable impact on an individual's life, even if he or she is subsequently exonerated.

An extreme illustration of the possible cost to the individual of participation in the judicial process is dramatically provided by the current debate surrounding Aboriginal deaths in custody. By the end of 1988, the Muirhead Royal Commission into deaths in custody was considering over 100 cases involving Aborigines who had died while in police lock-ups or in prison during the previous nine years. Many of these Aborigines were being held for trivial matters, such as failing to pay fines or breaching bail conditions. In a disturbing number of cases, no offence whatsoever had been committed. To cite just one example: an Aboriginal male died in a South Australian police cell in October 1987 soon after his removal by police from the casualty section of the local hospital for alleged intoxication. Although drunkenness in a public place is no longer an offence in this State, under the provisions of the *Public Intoxication Act* 1984 (S.A.) police have the right to detain persons in a safe place until they have sobered up. In this instance, the 'safe place' was the police lock-up.

The question of why so many Aborigines die in custody needs to be considered within the broader framework of why so many Aborigines are brought into the justice system in the first place, often for extremely trivial matters. At least some of the answers may be found through a close scrutiny of police and the use they make of their discretionary powers at the point of contact with an individual.

There is another reason for examining in detail the operation of police discretion at the point of entry into the criminal justice system. It is an undeniable fact that the police decision on *how* to apprehend a suspected young offender — whether by arrest or report — has important repercussions at later stages of the criminal justice process. For this reason also it is important to examine whether police exercise the power of arrest differently towards young Aborigines.

The history of relations between police and Aborigines is one of culpable beginnings followed by well-intentioned moves to ameliorate the problem through administrative initiatives. Aborigines have, since the first days of colonisation, been forced into frequent and often negative contact with police. As the main administrative arm of the government, police were given the contradictory roles of both punishing and protecting Aborigines as the frontiers of white settlement spread across the country. Police stations were established in. outlying areas to protect settlers from retaliatory action by the indigenous groups who were being dispossessed of their traditional lands. Yet once the settlers' position was secured, police became the agents for dispensing government rations to the small numbers of Aborigines who managed to survive the onslaught of European colonisation.

As white settlement spread through the arable areas of Australia, the Aboriginal remnants left in its wake were grouped together on small, segregated reserves run initially by missionary bodies and later, by government-appointed superintendents. Special legislation was enacted to control virtually every aspect of Aboriginal life, both on and off the reserves. Again, it was the police who were given responsibility for enforcing the often discriminatory and highly intrusive regulations.

Hence over the decades Aborigines have developed a deep-seated fear of and hostility towards police who have exerted so much control over their lives. This fear remains even amongst families now resident in the major cities to which they migrated in the 1950s and 1960s in search of a better environment where they could raise their children without the ever-present scrutiny of the white reserve managers and police.

In recognition of the continuing poor relationship between police and Aborigines, South Australia has, since the early 1970s, introduced a number of initiatives in this area. In 1972, a Police–Aboriginal Liaison Committee, consisting of representatives from the Police Department and the Aboriginal Legal Rights Movement, was set up to provide a 'regular and open forum in which Aborigines and police across the State could meet and discuss mutual concerns' (Bevan, 1984: 107). This was the first of its kind in Australia, pre-dating the Western Australian Special Cabinet Committee on Aboriginal–Police Relations by some four years and the New South Wales Police–Aboriginal Liaison Unit by eight years.

This was followed in 1975 by a set of guidelines issued by the South Australian Police Commissioner which not only contained a statement of official police policy towards Aborigines, but also laid down specific rules to be followed by police personnel 'with regard to Aboriginal people in their custody' (P.C.O. Circular No. 354, para. 1). Of particular relevance were the guidelines relating to the interrogation of Aborigines and the rights of Aboriginal prisoners (paras 7 and 8). These stipulated that when interrogating 'tribal or semi-tribal Aborigines' regarding a serious crime, police should make every effort 'to have an independent third party present at the interview', preferably either a solicitor or a field officer who had some understanding of the 'suspect's native language'. For urbanised Aborigines, police were under no obligation to ensure that a prisoner's friend be present but they were instructed not to obstruct an Aboriginal field officer attending the interrogation if 'the suspect requests such attendance' (para. 7).

These initiatives, in combination with the inception during the 1970s of special training courses for police officers designed to 'develop an insight into Aboriginal culture and lifestyle' ('Police–Aboriginal Relations Discussion Paper', 1984: 13), were hailed at the time of their introduction as 'the most progressive attempt to come to terms with this serious problem' (Clifford, 1981: 23).

Moves to improve police relations with Aborigines continued in the 1980s. Circular 354 was incorporated within Police General Orders and special provisions relating to the interrogation of Aboriginal children were introduced (Police General Order 3015.12) which required that a parent, guardian or an Aboriginal field officer should be present wherever possible during police questioning. In addition, it was stipulated that for children under the care of the Department for Community Welfare a departmental representative should be advised and be given the opportunity to be present during police questioning. These guidelines are additional to those which applied to the interviewing of children in general (General Order 3120.18.3).

A further initiative occurred in 1984 when, as part of its shift in emphasis towards community involvement in policing, a project team was set up by the Police Commissioner to look at police–Aboriginal relations. This investigation led to the establishment in 1985 of a Police Aide Scheme in selected Pitjantjatjara communities. Modelled on a similar scheme operating in the Northern Territory, it allows for specially trained Aboriginal aides to work with their own people 'to assist the police to provide a policing service that is suitable to those Aboriginal communities' (Pathe, 1985: 44).

Despite their apparently innovative nature, these programs have been the subject of serious criticism. For example, the guidelines governing the questioning of Aboriginal children apply only in the case of serious offences, rather than all matters. The Police–Aboriginal Liaison Committee is considered by many Aborigines to be an ineffective mechanism for initiating change, especially since it does not have the power to deal with specific complaints about police behaviour. The guidelines regarding interrogation procedures have also been criticised because of the lack of protection they afford to non-tribal Aborigines and the ease with which they can be circumvented or ignored by police.

Nor, it seems, has there been a noticeable improvement in Aboriginal attitudes towards law-enforcement personnel. In virtually every one of the interviews (Gale and Wundersitz, 1982) conducted with Aboriginal people living in Adelaide, specific examples of police discrimination against blacks were cited. Most adults in the Aboriginal community were able to recall at least one incident in which they or a close family member had been, at least according to their own perception of events, unjustly or harshly treated by police. Even though many of these stories cannot be verified, they help to perpetuate negative attitudes towards the police amongst young Aborigines and thus stimulate aggressive Aboriginal responses to police intervention.

The Decision to Apprehend

Police act as the crucial filter at the very first level of the justice system: they must decide whether to ignore certain behaviour, to issue an unofficial caution or to initiate criminal proceedings which will channel the young suspect into the formal justice process. A quantitative assessment of this crucial area of discretion is not possible because of a lack of data. In South Australia, no statistics are kept on the number of cautions issued or the circumstances which lead to this response; instead, available crime statistics deal exclusively with those individuals who have already been selected for official prosecution, while conveying no information whatsoever about those who have managed to avoid apprehension. Consequently, any assessment of whether police officers react differently to Aboriginal youths when deciding between an unofficial caution or formal proceedings must, of necessity, be based on non-statistical evidence. The following discussion therefore relies on observations of police behaviour, conducted primarily in Adelaide, and on material supplied by Aboriginal parents, young people and community workers which could subsequently be verified from independent sources.

During the course of the field work for this research, case after case emerged which brought into question the equity of police treatment of Aboriginal youth at the point of apprehension.

In discussions conducted with police officers, there were many statements to the effect that cautions were rarely, if ever, administered to young Aborigines. Instead, the preferred option was to prosecute. Some verification of this may be found in the types of offences with which some young Aborigines are charged. In one incident, seven young Aborigines in Adelaide were apprehended for stealing a pair of sandshoes. The charge: joint venture-larceny. In a second case, a house belonging to the State's Aboriginal housing agency was left vacant. Two Aboriginal children, aged ten and eleven years, entered the back yard and picked some oranges from a tree. They were each charged with larceny and being unlawfully on the premises, even though an Aboriginal community worker argued with police that not only had the previous occupants invited the children to 'help themselves' but also, because it was a designated Aboriginal house, the children regarded the fruit as being community property. In a third situation, a seventeen-year-old male was charged with being a 'minor consuming liquor' for taking a mouthful of drink from the glass of an adult. There was also the case of a twelve-year-old Aboriginal with no prior record of illegal behaviour who was arrested for being a 'suspected person'. Such a charge is normally reserved for individuals already convicted of certain offences who are observed by police in circumstances which bear some connection to their prior criminal activities.

All of these situations would seem to warrant a police caution rather than an apprehension. The fact that each case resulted in criminal proceedings raises fundamental questions about police treatment of Aborigines. If the children involved in these cases were middle-class whites, would police still apprehend them? More direct evidence that police responses vary according to the racial identity of the individuals involved is provided by the following incident, which was one of many brought to our notice. Two children, one Aboriginal and the other white, were intercepted stealing milk money by a milkman who called the police. When the officers arrived, they arrested the Aboriginal but cautioned the white youth and sent him home, in spite of the fact that the milkman said he was quite sure the white boy was the instigator and a regular offender.

Observations also revealed that at least some Aboriginal apprehensions resulted from police-initiated contact. For example, in one incident, members of the STAR Force, an elite tactical response group, 'raided' a house early one morning looking for an Aboriginal youth wanted on breaking and entering charges. They located a youth in the house, who tried to explain it was the wrong house, and that the police should be searching for his cousin who lived two streets away. When his explanation was ignored he started to abuse the officers and a scuffle broke out which resulted in his arrest for assaulting and hindering police. His mother, who was also at home at the time, entered into the argument and when police took her son away, she followed to the police station in her own car, stopping on the way to collect her husband at his place of employment. Arriving at the police station, both mother and father became embroiled in further altercations with the police until they too were arrested for using abusive language. In all, three members of the family were taken into custody as a result of a police raid on the wrong house.

In another case, an Aboriginal male, aged sixteen years, observed running down a street in the city, was stopped by police and asked why he was running. In response, he told the officers to mind their own 'fucking' business. The result: arrest for abusive language, with a secondary charge of resisting arrest. There was no evidence that he had committed any offence prior to being stopped for questioning. Instead, the officers apparently acted on the assumption that any Aboriginal youth observed running in a city street must be treated as a suspected offender.

Participant observations carried out in Hindley Street, the main entertainment centre of Adelaide and the night-time mecca for young people, have shown that police seem to stop and question Aborigines more often than other young people. The visibility of fairly large groups of Aborigines, coupled with the very high police presence in this area, clearly operates to the disadvantage of black youth. On many occasions during a Friday or Saturday evening it was possible to observe groups of young Aborigines walking along the footpath. Police would invariably stop them, ask their names and then check by radio for any outstanding warrants. If such a warrant had been issued, an immediate apprehension took place. Yet even if this was not the case, one or more of them would become aggressive, asking why they had been stopped when they had 'done nothing'. Before long, they would be arrested for using abusive language, assaulting police etc. By contrast, police questioning of groups of young whites occurred far less often. Moreover, if stopped, the whites appeared to be much more careful and respectful in the way they responded to questioning. After giving their names and addresses, they would be allowed to move on.

Police often justified the apprehension of young Aborigines on the ground that, when questioned, false names or addresses are given. In part, providing incorrect information may be a natural reaction by those wishing to avoid arrest for an outstanding warrant. Yet at times, the address supplied may be valid, even if it does not coincide with the information available to police from their computer records. Some young Aborigines, especially in Adelaide, are highly mobile, and move frequently from one relative's house to another. The address given at the time of questioning generally relates to their current residence, and may well differ from an address given a month previously. Police radio checks with their central computing files reveal such discrepancies and lead them to assume that a false address has been provided. In other situations, young Aborigines may simply be unable to give precise information, not because they do not have a 'fixed place of abode', but because they simply do not know the address. In our household surveys, we encountered this situation on a number of occasions. Often a family member living in one suburb of Adelaide could not give the actual address of a relative's house, yet was able to provide accurate directions on how to get there. For many Aborigines, where a person lives is perceived not in terms of a number or street name but as part of a broad, kin-based spatial network. The emphasis then is not on *where*, but *who* lives there and *how* to get to that person.

We have also observed a tendency for Aboriginal youths to run when they see a police car approaching. Although prompted by an expectation that they will be 'hassled', such a response inevitably arouses police suspicion and a chase almost always ensues, which usually results in the youths being charged. This fear of being 'hassled' is not unfounded, as the following examples illustrate. An Aboriginal youth, carrying a cassette recorder which he had recently purchased, was stopped and questioned by police about its ownership. He was allowed to go only when he was able to produce his receipt of purchase. The fact that he had the receipt with him was not fortuitous. His mother told us that she had insisted he carry it with him because of her fear that he would be questioned if, as an Aboriginal, he was seen with such an expensive piece of equipment. On another occasion, an Aboriginal male, aged sixteen years, was told he was being charged with 'tampering' after leaning against a parked car and running his hands along the outside while waiting for a break in the traffic so that he could cross a busy city street. The charge officially recorded was 'illegal interference to a motor vehicle' which is regarded as a relatively serious matter and for which he was subsequently sent to Court.

The treatment of Aboriginal youth could well benefit from some improvements in the application of police procedures. For example, police have the right to hold a person for a maximum period of four hours without laying any charges. This can be extended for another four hours if the permission of a justice of the peace is obtained. In one instance, police removed two young Aboriginal women from a city street at 11 p.m., on the grounds that they were at risk and that it was in their (i.e. the young women's) best interest to 'get them off the street'. However, these same young women were released some four hours later and found themselves back on the street at 3 a.m. with no way of getting home. Inevitably, this placed them at greater risk than did their previous situation. A number of mothers have also complained that they are not notified of their child's arrest until a considerable time (sometimes several days) has elapsed. This is reported to be so even for those families who have a telephone. This is contrary to Police General Order 3065.9.1 which states: 'Whenever a child is arrested, the arresting member must take steps to inform the parents or guardian of such child immediately.' Some youths were not informed of the charges laid against them at the time of arrest, or discovered subsequently that the charges recorded against them were different from those originally indicated. The number of such stories suggests either that police procedures need amendment or that existing procedures are not always adhered to in relation to Aboriginal youth.

Reliance on observational and case study material is obviously inadequate to prove that police systematically discriminate against Aboriginal youth when deciding whether or not to apprehend them and which charges to impose. Nevertheless, it does provide some evidence that not all officers exercise their discretionary powers equitably, whether because of personal bias or because of community pressure on them to react with obvious 'toughness' towards a group who are generally perceived by white mainstream society to be 'irresponsible', 'drunken', 'lazy' 'troublemakers' (Taft, 1970; Western, 1969; Wundersitz, 1979b).

The Method of Apprehension

Having decided to initiate criminal proceedings against a youth, the police must also decide on the appropriate method of apprehension: whether to arrest or report a suspect. In South Australia it is at this stage of the juvenile justice process that accurate analysis becomes possible because of the detailed records maintained on all young offenders. The remainder of this chapter then, deals with the question of whether race is or is not a critical factor in the police decision to arrest so many young Aborigines.

In this State, the statutory framework for the arrest of children is Section 42(2) of the *Children's Protection and Young Offenders Act*, 1979 (S.A.) which states that 'Any member of the police force may, without warrant, apprehend any child who is reasonably suspected of having committed an offence.' However, guidelines for the use of this power are found in police General Orders, which are made under Section 23 of the *Police Regulation Act* 1952 (S.A.). General Order 3065.1 stipulates that police

> should not exercise their power of arrest unless one or more of the following criteria exist, viz., there are reasonable grounds for belief that detention is necessary to:
> — ensure the appearance of the offender before a Court;
> — prevent the continuation or repetition of the offence; or
> — prevent the loss or destruction of evidence relating to the offence.

These statutory guidelines, which apply across all age groups, permit and indeed require the exercise of a considerable degree of discretion by police. Yet, in the specific case of children, additional directives have been introduced with the obvious intention of limiting this discretion and increasing the element of accountability to senior personnel. General Order 3065.8 specifically recommends that 'Unless there are particular reasons calling for immediate arrest, members will not arrest children where it appears the service of a summons would be sufficient to ensure the appearance of the defendant before a Court.' Moreover, if a decision is taken to arrest a child, then the police involved are required to obtain permission from commissioned officers prior to the arrest or, if this is not possible, then they must advise such commissioned officers of the reasons for the arrest 'as soon as practicable' thereafter.

These stipulations, clearly designed to minimise the use of arrest in relation to young people, accord with the overriding philosophy of the juvenile justice system which, in the name of welfare, seeks to protect and 'cushion' the child against the full impact of the law. Thus what would be considered appropriate treatment for an adult suspect is modified in the case of young offenders, in order to limit the disadvantage or damage arising from their contact with the criminal process.

Yet even with these additional safeguards, police officers in South Australia initiate proceedings against Aborigines in a manner which differentiates them from non-Aborigines. As noted in Chapter 3, members of this group are more likely than other young people to be arrested instead of being subjected to the alternative of a report. But is this because they are Aboriginal and are therefore the targets of racial prejudice? Or are other factors operating? American and British analyses of the relationship between race and police discretion suggest two alternative explanations. One draws attention to the different offending profile of blacks, and argues that their harsher treatment by police can be attributed to the fact that they have more serious charges laid against them and are more likely to possess a prior criminal record. The other explanation identifies as the critical factor the depressed socio-economic circumstances in which most black people live and argues that police react more severely towards particular classes of people rather than towards particular races.

To test whether such explanations are relevant in the South Australian context, two restrictions had to be imposed on the analysis: one temporal and one spatial. In contrast to the five-year study period employed in earlier chapters, one year only (1 July 1983–30 June 1984) was considered, in order to reduce the number of appearances to a level appropriate for the use of suitable statistical techniques. In addition, only those appearances which involved young people who were resident within the Adelaide Statistical Division at the time of apprehension were analysed. Since Aboriginal families resident in the city share essentially the same living environment as do non-Aboriginal city-dwellers, this locational restriction ensured some degree of uniformity in the two populations being compared.

Explaining the High Rate of Arrest Among Adelaide Aborigines

The disproportionate use of arrest for Aboriginal youth was as evident in Adelaide as in other parts of South Australia. During the one-year period selected for study, almost one-half (47.8 per cent) of all appearances by

Aboriginal youth living in the city were brought about by means of an arrest, compared with only 16.8 per cent of appearances by other Adelaide youth. In total, Aborigines accounted for 4.0 per cent of all appearances but they constituted 10.7 per cent of those appearances brought about by way of arrest. In contrast, they made up only 2.6 per cent of those appearances based on a police report.

There is then a strong statistical correlation between racial identity and the likelihood of being arrested. Yet such an association does not provide evidence of a causative link. The reason for an arrest may have nothing to do with whether or not a person is Aboriginal but instead may be due to other factors which also happen to vary along racial lines.

As already noted in Chapter 4, it was not only high arrest rates which set Aboriginal young offenders apart from other young offenders in South Australia. There were also substantial differences in the criminal profiles of the two groups as well as differences in their socio-economic and residential characteristics. This applied equally to that group being investigated here: namely those Aborigines and non-Aborigines resident in Adelaide at the time of their apprehension. More specifically, young Adelaide Aborigines were more likely to be charged with serious crimes such as vehicle theft and break, enter, steal and less likely to be charged with minor offences such as shoplifting than were city-based non-Aboriginal youth. They were also more likely to have multiple counts laid against them, to possess prior records of appearances before both Aid Panels and the Children's Court and were more likely to appear in Court as absconders or while under an existing order. Although there were no obvious age or sex differences between the two groups, Aboriginal youth resident in Adelaide at the time of apprehension were more likely to be unemployed and were more likely to come from non-nuclear families than their non-Aboriginal counterparts. In fact, almost one-half of the Aboriginal appearances in Adelaide during the one-year study period involved unemployed young people, compared with less than one-quarter of the non-Aboriginal appearances. Youth from a nuclear family situation accounted for only 26.5 per cent of all Aboriginal appearances in Adelaide, but 65.1 per cent of non-Aboriginal appearances. Furthermore, proportionately more Aboriginal than non-Aboriginal appearances involved youth from the poorer socio-economic areas of the city.

These differences are not only interesting in their own right, but also may have a bearing on the question of why so many young Aborigines are arrested. In fact, the legal, socio-economic and residential factors on which Aborigines and non-Aborigines differed so markedly were precisely those same characteristics which, when subjected to further statistical testing, proved to be significantly related to the police decision to arrest. There was, for example, a clear association between the likelihood of arrest and the nature of the offence[1] (see Appendix 2). Street crimes, such as disorderly behaviour, were linked with high arrest rates, as were the property offences of break and enter with intent, vehicle theft and break, enter, steal. At the other end of the scale, the minor property offence of shoplifting was associated with an extremely low rate of arrest.

A significant relationship was also found between the number of offence charges and the mode of apprehension (see Appendix 3). Relatively low arrest rates were recorded in those cases where only one charge count was involved but as the number of charges increased, so did the likelihood of arrest. A similar pattern emerged when prior appearance records were considered. Young people who had not previously come before either an Aid Panel or the Children's Court were less likely to be arrested than were those who had made at least one prior appearance. As the number of previous hearings increased, so did the likelihood of arrest.

This association between the outcomes of police discretion and those legal factors which comprise the criminal profile of a young offender was expected, as were the findings that older youth were more likely to be arrested than younger youth and males were more likely to be arrested than females (see Appendix 4). However, it was not anticipated that a significant relationship would be found between the socio-economic variables and the mode of apprehension. It was surprising, for example, to find that arrest rates varied substantially according to the family structure within which the individual lived at the time of apprehension, with youth from nuclear families recording the lowest arrest rates. In fact, only 9.3 per cent of appearances by youth living with both parents were based on arrest. This contrasted with 17.7 per cent of those from single-parent households and 26.1 per cent of those living with relatives or foster parents. Employment status also co-varied with the method of apprehension. One-third of appearances by unemployed young offenders were arrest-based, compared with only 18.1 per cent of those cases involving employed youth.

Finally, the address of the individual at the time of apprehension was also associated with the likelihood of arrest. Police officers maintain that all persons with no fixed place of abode are automatically arrested to ensure their attendance at Court, the assumption being that they would be unable to locate a young person with no stable contact address five or six weeks hence to serve him or her with a summons. However, all but a few of the youth apprehended in the city during the study period had a specific address recorded on their files. Very few were listed as having 'no fixed place of abode'. Further discussions with police revealed that, even if a person was able to give an address (which was duly entered into the records) it was left to the discretion of the officer to determine whether that address was 'fixed' or not. For example, if a young Aboriginal gave the address of an 'aunt' with whom he or she was staying, the apprehending officer might decide, either through prior knowledge or subjective judgement, to treat this as 'no fixed place of abode'. (An aunt, in the Aboriginal context, has a much broader definition than a sister of one's mother or father.) There is a definite discrepancy, then, between the actual information recorded on file and the police assessment of that information. Youth listed in the records as residing at a particular address may, in fact, be treated by police as homeless and, therefore, appropriate candidates for arrest.

Even in those situations where the addresses provided by those questioned were judged to be 'fixed', there was still a connection between place of residence and the method of apprehension. In the lower socio-economic areas of the city, the proportion of apprehensions based on arrest was higher than the Adelaide average; conversely, in the relatively prestigious suburbs, the proportion of arrests was well below the Adelaide average (see Appendix 4). Aboriginal youth may therefore be doubly disadvantaged here. Not only is the validity of their address more often questioned by the authorities because of their high residential mobility within an extended kin network, but they also live in those areas of the city where recorded arrest rates are high. Such findings argue cogently in favour of socio-economic bias, but not necessarily for the operation of specific racial bias.

Clearly then, Aboriginal and non-Aboriginal youth who are brought into the justice system differ on those same legal, socio-economic and residential characteristics which also seem to have some bearing on the method of apprehension. Consequently, it may be these differences rather than racial identity *per se* which explain the obvious disparity in treatment accorded these two groups by law-enforcement officers. More specifically, it is possible that Aboriginal youth may be arrested in disproportionate numbers not because they are Aboriginal but because they possess certain criminal profiles or social characteristics which, for various reasons, attract high arrest rates.

How relevant, then, is the issue of racial identity to the decision to arrest, and how much is it due to the disproportionate numbers of Aborigines who fit into these other categories which have a high risk of arrest? If the legal, socio-economic and residential differences between Aboriginal and non-Aboriginal young offenders could be eliminated, would the two groups still be apprehended differently?

Most attempts to explain high Aboriginal arrest rates have in the past focused primarily on the nature of the crime. Eggleston (1976: 27), for example, claimed that the high proportion of Aboriginal arrests which she observed could be attributed to the fact that Aborigines were charged with different offences to whites. Yet this single-factor explanation was not borne out by an analysis of Adelaide young offenders. Even when controlling for differences between Aborigines and non-Aborigines by comparing only those apprehended for the same offence, major discrepancies in arrest rates persisted. For example, 93.3 per cent of all Aboriginal appearances involving disorderly or offensive behaviour as the major charge were initiated by means of arrest, compared with only 48.2 per cent of all non-Aboriginal appearances for this same offence. Similarly, 47.8 per cent of all Aboriginal appearances involving the charge of break, enter, steal were by way of arrest, compared with only 37.7 per cent of the non-Aboriginal appearances.

Large differences in the method of apprehension also persisted when comparisons were made between Aborigines and non-Aborigines charged with the same number of offences, or who had similar records of appearances before either Aid Panels or the Children's Court. Similarly, controlling separately for employment status or family structure or residential address failed to account for the disproportionate use of arrest for young Aborigines. Even when comparing Aboriginal and non-Aboriginal youth resident in the same suburb of Adelaide, the former were still proportionately more likely to be brought into the juvenile justice system by way of an arrest than were other young people. To illustrate, 57.9 per cent of all Aboriginal appearances involving youths resident in the Local Government Area of Enfield were based on arrest, compared with only 21.3 per cent of the non-Aboriginal appearances by youths from the same area.

Thus no one factor could adequately account for the marked disparity in the method of apprehension applied by police to Aboriginal and non-Aboriginal youth. Appendix 5 provides statistical verification of the persistence of a strong link between Aboriginality and the use of arrest, no matter which area of difference between the two groups, whether it be legal, socio-economic or residential, was separately controlled for. Clearly, the single-cause approach adopted by previous researchers does little to disprove the argument that police operate in a racially biased manner towards Aborigines. In fact, it supports that view. Yet such an approach, of testing for the effects of one factor only on the relationship between identity and the method of apprehension, is open to serious criticism. It is not only statistically simplistic but it also fails to come to grips with the complexities of police decision-making. It does not allow for the fact that, in selecting an appropriate response to a particular situation, police may take into account not just one but a number of interrelated factors. Thus, if we look just at the nature of the crime, a discriminatory police response is still indicated. However, if the nature of the crime is considered in conjunction with other legal and socio-economic factors, more equitable treatment may emerge.

This, in fact, proved to be the case for Adelaide youth. When differences in the criminal, socio-economic and residential characteristics of young Aborigines and non-Aborigines were simultaneously taken into account, in general it was found that Aboriginal youth no longer faced a greater probability of being arrested.

Table 5.1 details the method of apprehension applied to selected Aboriginal and non-Aboriginal young offenders who have been carefully

Table 5.1:   Mode of apprehension for the matched group of Aboriginal and non-Aboriginal appearances

Mode of Apprehension	Aborigines		Non-Aborigines	
	n	%	n	%
Arrest	119	43.6	60	22.0
Non-arrest	154	56.4	213	78.0
Total	273	100.0	273	100.0

matched to eliminate socio-economic differences between the two groups. To achieve this matching, for each[2] of the 273 appearances by Adelaide-based Aborigines apprehended during the twelve-month period, a non-Aboriginal appearance was selected which possessed exactly the same characteristics of age, gender, occupation, family structure and residence (Appendix 6 discusses the matching process in more detail). Yet even when comparisons are narrowed to these two carefully matched groups, substantial differences in the method of police apprehension for Aborigines and non-Aborigines are still evident. In fact, 43.6 per cent of the 273 Aboriginal cases considered were based on arrest, yet only 22.0 per cent of the matched 273 non-Aboriginal cases involved this method of apprehension. The ominous conclusion is that young Aborigines who possess the same social, residential and demographic characteristics as a group of non-Aboriginal youth are still significantly more likely to be arrested. On the basis of these findings, the possibility that racial discrimination is operating at the point of police apprehension still cannot be discounted.

The process of matching the 273 Aboriginal appearances with 273 non-Aboriginal appearances eliminated any socio-economic and residential differences, but it did not consider the criminal records of these two paired groups. Yet Table 5.2 shows a substantial disparity in the offending profiles even between matched Aboriginal and non-Aboriginal youth. It is clear that urban Aborigines living a similar lifestyle to other city-dwelling young people also in poor economic circumstances are still charged differently and have different criminal histories. As indicated in the table, the 273 Aborigines were proportionately more likely to be charged with the serious property offences of break, enter, steal and vehicle theft whereas the matched group of 273 non-Aborigines were more likely to be apprehended for the minor property offences of shoplifting or larceny. The former were also significantly more likely to have multiple charges laid against them and to have a record of prior appearances before both Aid Panels and the Children's Court. This finding raises a large number of questions, which cannot be dealt with here, as to why the records of Aboriginal youth are so different from those of other youth living in very similar circumstances. But more importantly for this study, it introduces the possibility that these differences in charge patterns could account for the persistent differences between the two matched groups in arrest rates.

A second matching, using not only the five socio-economic variables but also the legal variables of the major charge, number of offence charges, number of previous Aid Panel appearances and number of previous Children's Court appearances,[3] could not be used to answer this question because from amongst the 5995 'useful' non-Aboriginal appearance records, only 92 were identified which exactly fitted an Aboriginal appearance. This means that some two-thirds of all young Aborigines brought into the juvenile justice system during the twelve-month study period possessed specific combinations of socio-economic and offending characteristics which were not duplicated by any of the 5995 non-Aborigines apprehended during the same time period. This confirms the fact that as a whole, Aboriginal and non-Aboriginal youth offenders differ

Table 5.2: A comparison of the offending profiles of the 273 Aboriginal and 273 matched non-Aboriginal appearances

Offending profile	Aborigines %	Non-Aborigines %
Major charge		
Larceny	8.1	16.1
Break, enter, steal	23.1	13.6
Vehicle theft	15.7	7.7
Assault	9.9	2.9
Disorderly behaviour	5.1	2.2
Shoplifting	8.8	28.6
Other	29.3	28.9
Total	100.0	100.0
Number of offence charges		
1	50.2	68.1
2	23.8	17.6
3 or more	26.0	14.3
Total	100.0	100.0
Number of previous Aid Panel appearances		
0	39.9	70.3
1–2	27.8	16.1
3 or more	32.3	13.6
Total	100.0	100.0
Number of previous Court appearances		
0	29.0	53.5
1–2	32.2	32.2
3 or more	38.8	14.3
Total	100.0	100.0

substantially not only along socio-economic and residential lines, but also in terms of their criminal records. This is not necessarily an indication that they actually offend differently, but it certainly demonstrates the enormous differences in charges laid against them and how often they come to official notice.

Since there were such a limited number of cases where matching across the full range of factors was possible, it was not valid to investigate the potential impact on the arrest decision of differences in legal profiles through the process of pairing 'like' appearances. Therefore, an alternative approach based on logistic regression analysis[4] was adopted.

The 273 Aboriginal and 273 non-Aboriginal appearances previously matched according to socio-economic criteria were each subjected to logistic regression analysis (see Appendix 7). This methodology allows us to identify whether each of the four legal factors (major charge, number of offence charges, number of previous Court and Aid Panel appearances) contributes independently, in statistical terms, to the decision to arrest. A factor will only be retained in the statistical model if it makes a contribution over and above that of the other three factors being analysed. Applying this analysis to the Aboriginal group, each of the four legal factors was retained. This suggests that when deciding whether to arrest a young person, police may be influenced, whether consciously or otherwise, by the nature and number of offence charges and his or her prior appearance record. The same result was obtained for the matched group of non-Aboriginal appearances. The implications of these findings are as follows: Aboriginal and non-Aboriginal youth who possess similar demographic, socio-economic and residential characteristics nevertheless exhibit different charge profiles. In turn, these different charge profiles play a role in the decision to arrest. It seems then, that the very high arrest rates observed for Aboriginal youth can largely be explained by differences in charge patterns and socio-economic characteristics, rather than by invoking the argument of racial bias.

To explore this further, the logistic regression procedure was again used to generate probability tables, firstly for the Aboriginal and then for the matched non-Aboriginal group. Each table (Appendixes 8 and 9) depicts the likelihood of an arrest for every possible combination of the major charge, number of offence counts, prior Aid Panel records and prior Court records. By comparing the values generated for the Aboriginal group with the corresponding values produced for the non-Aboriginal group, it is possible to determine whether Aboriginal and non-Aboriginal youth, already pre-matched on socio-economic criteria, were equally likely to be arrested when differences in their legal profiles were also eliminated.

A surprising picture emerged from this analysis. Comparison revealed that the predicted probability of arrest for Aboriginal appearances was generally lower, and in some instances dramatically so, than that of non-Aboriginal appearances for most combinations of the four legal variables. For example, young Aborigines charged with assault as the only offence, and with a record of at least three prior Aid Panel and three prior Court appearances, were predicted as having 45 chances in 100 of being arrested. A non-Aboriginal with exactly the same offending profile had an estimated 50 chances in 100 of being arrested. In some cases, the differences were substantial. To illustrate, in cases where the single charge of disorderly behaviour was combined with at least three prior Court appearances but no previous Aid Panel appearance, the predicted likelihood of an arrest was 41 chances in 100 if the person was Aboriginal, but 89 chances in 100 if non-Aboriginal. Large differences were evident right across the board for this particular offence.

One of the few situations in which the logistic regression model did predict that Aboriginal youth had a consistently higher probability of arrest than non-Aboriginal youth, once both socio-economic and legal differences between the two groups had been taken into account, was in relation to the major charge of vehicle theft. This applied irrespective of the number of prior appearances and the number of offence charges laid.

For example, when an offender was charged with a single offence and had no prior Aid Panel or Court appearance record, then the probability of being arrested for a charge of vehicle theft was 14 chances in 100 if that person was Aboriginal, but only 4 chances per 100 if non-Aboriginal. Similarly, when one offence charge was combined with three or more previous Panel *and* three or more previous Court appearances, then the chances of being arrested was almost 63 per 100 for Aborigines but only 37 per 100 for non-Aborigines.

According to these probability tables, then, there is no statistical evidence to suggest that racial discrimination against Aborigines is prevalent at this point of police decision-making once the charges have been determined and prior records have been taken into account. If anything, the situation has been reversed, with Aboriginal youth now predicted as having a lower probability of being apprehended by way of an arrest than non-Aboriginal youth from a similar urban background. This suggests, somewhat surprisingly, that young Aborigines are in fact receiving more lenient treatment from police. However, it must be emphasised that these findings emerge only when comparing the whole Aboriginal offending population with an extremely small sub-group of non-Aboriginal offenders — a sub-group which is totally unrepresentative of the non-Aboriginal offending population as a whole.

When all Aboriginal appearances are compared with all non-Aboriginal appearances, rather than with a carefully selected sub-group, the legal differences evident between the two matched groups are augmented by considerable differences in socio-demographic and residential character-istics. The question then is: do the socio-economic factors themselves make a contribution to the arrest decision over and above that of the legal factors?

To test this, logistic regression analysis incorporating both legal as well as socio-economic characteristics as independent variables was per-formed firstly on all Aboriginal appearances and then on all 6000 or so non-Aboriginal appearances.[5] The aim was to determine whether age, gender, family structure, occupational status and residential address played any role in the arrest decision.

The results (Appendix 10) showed that for the Aboriginal group, occupational status and gender were retained in the analysis, thereby indicating that both made a significant contribution to the arrest decision which was additional to that made by the legal factors. Thus, irrespective of the nature of the offence, the number of offence charges or the individual's prior record, the fact of being male and unemployed does apparently increase the likelihood of being arrested rather than reported by police. Moreover, although both factors significantly improved the model's ability to predict an arrest outcome, occupation was the most important of the two, accounting for 75.7 per cent of the total improve-ment. The other factors of age, family structure and residential address were all excluded, indicating that they made no significant contribution to the arrest decision over and above that provided by the other factors tested.

For non-Aboriginal youth, the three factors of occupational status, family structure and age were included in the step-wise logistic regression procedure (Appendix 10), indicating that all contributed significantly to the arrest decision. Again, occupation proved to be the most important, accounting for 71.0 per cent of the total improvement in the model's ability to predict an arrest. Both sex and residential address were excluded. These results highlight the role played by socio-economic factors in the operation of police discretion.

Quite apart from the expected influence exerted on the arrest decision by offence characteristics, it is evident that socio-economic factors and occupational status in particular also contribute to this decision-making process for Aborigines and non-Aborigines alike. Yet, although the association between employment and the decision to arrest has important ramifications for all youth, it is particularly relevant for young Aborigines since such a high proportion of this group are unemployed. Inevitably the weight accorded to such socio-economic factors militates against fair treatment for Aborigines.

Summary

That Aborigines experience disproportionately high rates of arrest has often been attributed to the fact that they live predominantly in remote, spatially separate communities and exhibit marked cultural differences. Yet even when eliminating these differences by comparing only Aboriginal and non-Aboriginal youth resident in Adelaide, substantial disparities in arrest patterns were still evident. This suggests that explanations couched in locational and cultural terms are inadequate.

Yet statistical analysis indicated that these high arrest rates could be attributed only minimally to the operation of racial bias. Instead, two sets of factors, one legal and the other socio-economic, emerged as the prime determinants of the differentially high rates of arrest experienced by Aboriginal youth. Such findings raise other questions.

Whilst charge profiles seem to provide a justification for arrest patterns, why do the charge profiles of Aboriginal youth vary so greatly from those of their non-Aboriginal counterparts even when comparisons are restricted to those who possess the same socio-economic characteristics and live in the same urban environment? The charges laid against a suspect may be as much the product of police discretion as is the decision to arrest and there is no reason to suppose that either is conclusively determined by the real pattern of offending behaviour. Thus, the observed variations in charge patterns may indicate police discrimination at the pre-arrest stage. Although this cannot be ascertained from official data, the case study material presented in the first part of this chapter throws some light on the issue. What on the surface seems a valid police response to a particular person's behaviour may actually conceal discriminatory practices. Indeed, the primary shortcoming of officially recorded crime statistics is that there is no reason to assume that they accurately reflect actual patterns of offending behaviour. McCorquodale (1980: 54) makes the telling comment that what crime statistics reveal is interesting, 'but what they conceal is vital'. Since there is little evidence of overt discrimination being shown to Aborigines once the charges have been laid, any changes to existing legislation would in no way lessen the over-representation of Aboriginal youth in the arrest profiles.

A second set of factors operates against Aborigines. This relates to their lower socio-economic status. In the youth offending population as a whole, unemployment proved to be strongly associated with the likelihood of arrest, irrespective of a young person's criminal profile or other social characteristics. A substantially larger proportion of Aborigines than non-Aborigines were unemployed. As a result, disproportionately large numbers of Aborigines are being arrested because they are unemployed, irrespective of their criminal records. In addition, it was shown that the residential household arrangements influence the police decision to arrest. Young people who do not live in nuclear households tend to be arrested because of their living arrangements, irrespective of the offence charges laid. The employed child from a middle-class nuclear household is less likely to be arrested than an unemployed child living in an extended household.

The only explanation which can be offered for these findings lies in the special directive issued to police that, in the case of children, an arrest should be used primarily to ensure the appearance of the accused before the Court. It is possible that police act on the assumption that young persons who have left school and are without a job, or who do not have both parents at home to act as supports, will be 'bad risks' for the report procedure: that is, they will not obey a summons and appear in Court under their own volition. The use of such criteria in the decision-making process has serious implications for Aboriginal youth. The greater prevalence of so-called 'problem' family backgrounds amongst young Aboriginal offenders results, it seems, in a greater tendency by police to perceive them as 'bad risks' which, in turn, contributes to their greater likelihood of being arrested rather than reported.

The use, whether intentional or otherwise, of such socio-economic criteria in the decision-making process requires reappraisal because it penalises individuals for factors which bear no direct relationship to the offending behaviour itself but are designed primarily to enable the processing of these juveniles to proceed more smoothly. Moreover, the whole concept of 'good risk' and 'bad risk' groups is arguably built on erroneous stereotypes. Being unemployed does not necessarily render a person unreliable; nor does coming from a single-parent family mean that a child will not have parental support or discipline.

By contrast, some of these characteristics may in reality be of positive value to the individuals involved. This is particularly true in relation to residential mobility. A detailed study of Aboriginal households in Adelaide (Gale and Wundersitz, 1982) indicated that these households moved frequently from one rented house to another until they had succeeded in locating close to kin. This provided the much-needed security of access to a family support network in times of economic or personal difficulty. The movement of young people from one house to another within this neighbouring kin network reflects the operation of extended family support. Yet police consider high residential mobility as a clear indicator that the individual has no fixed place of abode, and is therefore an appropriate target for arrest to ensure attendance in Court.

Decisions based on socio-economic criteria discriminate not only against Aborigines but against all young people who are already disadvantaged by their depressed status within the community. This operates in direct opposition to the welfare concerns of the juvenile justice system, which aims to assist, rather than to penalise, young people 'in need'.

Whatever the reasons for an arrest, whether it be overt police discrimination at the point of charging (which cannot be demonstrated) or more general community social prejudice (which can be proven), arrest is of itself an occurrence of considerable significance for the young person involved, since it appears to have a marked effect on the way a case will proceed through subsequent stages of the juvenile justice process. The next chapter demonstrates that the force of the decision to arrest is by no means spent at the time of entry into the formal criminal process, but has repercussions on the Screening Panel decisions and even at later stages. The implications for young Aborigines who are arrested in disproportionate numbers are obvious.

6

Diversion or Trial: Who Decides?

In criminal justice systems which utilise formal diversionary procedures as the alternative to ordinary trial in Court, the determination of which route a case is to take is of crucial significance to the alleged offender. South Australia has a developed system of diversion, represented by the existence of Children's Aid Panels which, as noted earlier, have operated since 1972. Their objective is to achieve a positive effect on a child's future conduct and so reduce the likelihood of further offending. In South Australia since 1979 Screening Panels have operated as the all-important pre-trial 'sieve' in the juvenile justice process, deciding which cases are or are not suitable for diversion. This chapter, which examines how this sieve operates, suggests that Screening Panels do not give Aboriginal youth opportunities equal to those afforded to their non-Aboriginal counterparts to benefit from the system of diversion. This can largely be attributed to the fact that the police decision taken at the first level of the juvenile justice process to arrest rather than report a child exerts an extremely strong influence on the Screening Panel's referral decision.

The right of Screening Panels to consider cases where a young person has been arrested as well as those where a young person has been reported is a legislative change from the earlier *Juvenile Courts Act* 1971, under which all those arrested were ineligible for diversion to Juvenile Aid Panels and had to appear in the Juvenile Court. Yet analysis suggests that this legislative change, made with the well-intentioned aim of offering a wider range of children the opportunity to receive the positive benefits of a Children's Aid Panel appearance, has not in practice achieved the desired effect. Once again it seems that good legislative intentions have in reality failed to deliver social justice.

A Screening Panel is composed of a police officer and an officer from the Department for Community Welfare. These Panels exist throughout

South Australia and usually meet in a Department for Community Welfare office, although in country areas in particular, screenings may be done by telephone. Matters involving children who have been reported are considered at ordinary Screening Panel meetings, which occur about once a week in urban areas but less frequently in the country. However, in the case of an arrest, since the young person involved must appear in the Children's Court within one working day of his or her apprehension, a special Screening Panel is convened that morning to decide whether the case should be sent to Court.

Screening Panels, like any other bodies acting under the *Children's Protection and Young Offenders Act* 1979, are bound by the general policy of section 7 of that Act. Of crucial importance in the decision-making process are the guidelines developed by the Police Department and the Department for Community Welfare for their officers who sit on Screening Panels. The guidelines of both those departments identify the seriousness of the alleged offence, the offender's past record and the existence of a Court order as considerations relevant to referral to the Children's Court. In addition, the police guidelines refer to the young person's need for assessment and are more specific as to the past record: two or more previous appearances before an Aid Panel should usually result in referral to Court.

Neither a child nor his or her parent has any right to appear before a Screening Panel, nor to make representations to it. There is no right of appeal against its decision. Although Screening Panels are not judicial in character, nevertheless they are statutory bodies whose decisions affect rights. Their composition and procedure can be criticised on several counts. Firstly, the police member of a Screening Panel could be viewed as both judge and prosecutor in the one matter. In Scotland, where the system of Children's Hearings is comparable in some ways[1] with South Australia's Aid Panels, 'access to the system is controlled exclusively by reporters' (Sinclair, 1982: 24)[2] — independent officials appointed by local council authorities. Reporters enjoy autonomy in the decision as to whether individuals need the formal State intervention of a Children's Hearing. Secondly, a child is given no opportunity to put arguments to a Screening Panel, either personally or through a lawyer. He or she is not notified of the Panel's meeting, nor (at this stage) of the allegations against him or her. Finally, there is no appeal from the decision of a Screening Panel and indeed, no obvious way in which that decision could be challenged, despite the fact that it has an important effect on legal rights.[3]

In favour of Screening Panels it can be argued that the decision about the appropriate procedural future of a case must be taken at an early stage, and that discretion is preferable to arbitrary and inflexible statutory criteria. Nichols (1985: 232) stresses the positive aspects of the Screening Panel's composition:

> . . . The police have always had the discretion of whether or not to proceed with the prosecution of offenders. The Screening Panel enables a social work

perspective to be added at this decision-making point, and although there are faults, on balance the Screening Panels do provide the authorities with the opportunity of responding to the needs of each individual case within some general guidelines.

Thus Screening Panels make the crucial decision whether or not a case should go to Court. A Court appearance is obviously a much more serious matter for a child than an appearance before an Aid Panel. The former is not only more stigmatising, but also affords less opportunity for constructive counselling of the child with the aim of preventing further offending.

Yet, at this all-important stage of the pre-trial process, there are very marked differences in referral patterns between Aboriginal and non-Aboriginal youth. Throughout South Australia, a disproportionately large number of Aboriginal children are referred to Court, and are thus not given the opportunity to profit from the positive counselling that Aid Panels provide. Children's Aid Panels were created with the primary aim of preventing further offending. All the more disturbing then, is the finding that one group appears to be denied equitable access to them. At no stage in the juvenile justice process, from the first point of apprehension to the ultimate stage of sentencing, are differences in outcome between Aborigines and non-Aborigines more critical.

It is, therefore, not surprising that young Aborigines consider themselves to be discriminated against by Screening Panels and often give examples of specific instances of such treatment. Because the official records seem to support this perception, it is important to establish whether in fact there is racial bias operating in these pre-trial 'sifting' mechanisms, or whether factors other than racial identity explain the differential rates of Court referrals for Aboriginal and non-Aboriginal youth.

To test how Screening Panels operate for young Aborigines, it is again necessary to limit the analysis to one year only, July 1983–June 1984, and to those young people resident in Adelaide at the time of apprehension so that cultural or lifestyle differences are minimised. Even within this Westernised, urban population, a disproportionately large number of appearances by Aborigines were referred to Court rather than to Aid Panels. During the study period, 74.4 per cent of cases involving Adelaide-based Aborigines were referred to Court, compared with 35.6 per cent of non-Aboriginal appearances. These differences in referral outcomes are substantial and suggest that this pre-trial mechanism, specially set up in 1979 to ensure greater equity in the operation of juvenile justice, functions in an apparently disadvantageous manner, even for Aborigines living a completely Westernised lifestyle in an urban environment.

In deciding the procedural future of a case, Screening Panels exercise a considerable degree of discretion and, as already noted, investigating the exercise of such discretionary powers is fraught with difficulty. However, because Panels operate under guidelines from two departments their discretion is not unfettered. Furthermore, they have access to information about the social background and to the legal records of any young offender whose case they are considering.

Given the emphasis in these guidelines on the offending behaviour itself, it was scarcely surprising to find a statistical correlation between the criminal profile and the Screening Panel's referral decision. As shown in Appendix 11, a relatively high proportion of young people charged with serious property offences, such as vehicle theft or break, enter, steal, were sent to the Children's Court, while in contrast, no cases involving shoplifting recorded such an outcome. The so-called 'street offences' also attracted high Court appearance rates. Screening Panels were also significantly more likely to order a Court appearance for an individual who was charged with multiple counts and who had a prior record of appearance either before an Aid Panel or the Children's Court (Appendix 12). As the number of offence charges or previous appearances increased, so did the likelihood of the current appearance being directed to Court.

It was surprising, however, to find a significant relationship between the referral patterns and the method of apprehension. As noted at the start of this chapter, a legislative change was made in 1979 so that all individuals, including those who had been arrested, became in theory eligible for diversion to an Aid Panel. Despite this, whether or not a young person had been arrested correlated very strongly with the decision to refer to Court. An overwhelming 94.7 per cent of cases initiated by way of arrest were dealt with by the Children's Court, compared with only 24.5 per cent of all cases initiated by a report. It is possible that the change introduced by legislation in 1979 may have proved quite ineffectual in practice.

Yet it was not only the criminal profile which correlated with the referral decision. When Screening Panel outcomes were tested against the socio-economic characteristics of the alleged offenders, some predictable, albeit unfortunate results emerged (Appendix 13). Since one of the main functions of any pre-trial decision-making process is to keep young children away from the formal Court system for as long as possible, it was not unexpected to find a significant relationship between age and the referral outcome such that as age increased, so did the proportion of appearances referred to the Children's Court. Males were also more likely to be referred to Court than females.

The social background factors of family structure, occupational status and place of residence also showed a strong correlation with Screening Panel decisions. Young people living in a normative nuclear-family situation, for example, were less likely to be referred to Court. In fact, only 22.4 per cent of appearances involving youths from two-parent families went to Court, compared with 37.7 per cent of all appearances by persons from a single-parent family, 47.5 per cent of all appearances by individuals living with foster parents or relatives, and 66.1 per cent of all appearances by those living in hostels or who were flatting or living with friends. Being unemployed was also linked to high rates of Court referral. Screening Panels directed only 18.3 per cent of students to the Children's Court, compared with 40.3 per cent of all employed persons, and a high

62.0 per cent of unemployed youth. Finally, young people living in areas of lower socio-economic status, such as the inner city region of Adelaide and the older residential industrial areas to the west and north-west of the city, had relatively high rates of Court referral, whereas those from the higher-status areas of the eastern foothills had low Court referral rates. Although these results were expected, they raise serious questions concerning the equity of decision-making.

Since all of the above characteristics (with the exception of age and gender) correlate not only with referral outcomes but also with racial identity, this raises the possibility that racial bias does not directly influence the decision-making process. Instead, it could be argued that Aborigines are being treated differently by Screening Panels either because of their different criminal profiles or their depressed socio-economic circumstances or both. In attempting to test this, the methods outlined in the previous chapter to analyse differences between Aboriginal and non-Aboriginal youth in police arrest rates were applied.

Again it was clear that when controlling separately for any one of the legal or socio-economic differences previously found to exist between Aboriginal and non-Aboriginal young offenders, substantial disparities in the percentage of cases referred to Court still remained (see discussion and results in Appendix 14). Yet it is probable that the Screening Panel's decision on the appropriateness of a Court or Aid Panel appearance is based not on any single factor but on a combination of issues.

To investigate whether a group of Aboriginal appearances and a selected sub-group of non-Aboriginal appearances involving individuals who possess the same socio-economic, residential and demographic characteristics still differ in their pattern of Screening Panel referrals, the same matched groups identified in Chapter 5 were used here. The findings were dramatic. Even when comparing Aborigines and non-Aborigines who possess the same characteristics of age, gender, family structure, occupational status and residential address, the two groups still recorded totally dissimilar patterns of referral. Substantially more Aborigines than non-Aborigines continued to be directed to the Children's Court. In fact, 68.9 per cent of Aboriginal appearances were referred to Court, compared with only 38.5 per cent of the socio-economically matched non-Aboriginal appearances. Even when socio-economic differences are eliminated, the differential treatment accorded Aborigines by Screening Panels remains.

However, it is not sufficient to have regard only to socio-economic factors for, as was pointed out in the last chapter, the two matched groups still possess quite different legal profiles or offending histories. To assess whether these legal differences could explain the persistent differences in the referral outcomes, logistic regression analysis was applied firstly to the Aboriginal group of 273 appearances and then to the matched non-Aboriginal group.[4]

For the 273 Aboriginal appearances, four of the five legal factors entered as independent variables were retained in the analysis: the major charge, number of previous Aid Panel appearances, number of previous

Children's Court appearances, and the method of apprehension. This suggests that each of these makes a contribution to the referral decision which is additional to that made by the other legal variables tested. The only factor excluded was the number of offence charges. The findings concerning the major charge and the individual's previous Aid Panel and Court appearance records are consistent with the guidelines of the police and the Department for Community Welfare, which specify the seriousness of the alleged offence and the child's prior criminal record as considerations relevant to the referral decision. However, the mode of apprehension does not appear at all in those guidelines; it was in fact purposely removed from the legislation in 1979.

For the matched 273 non-Aboriginal appearances, four of the five legal variables were also retained in the step-wise logistic regression analysis. These were the major charge, number of offence charges, number of previous Court appearances and method of apprehension. The number of previous Aid Panel appearances was excluded, thereby indicating that it made no contribution to the referral decision over and above that accounted for by the other four legal variables. Its rejection is unexpected, given its specific mention in Screening Panel guidelines. So in at least two areas Screening Panels operate differently in practice from the intention of the legislation.

It is also difficult to explain why a different legal variable was excluded for the non-Aboriginal group than for the Aboriginal group. Our findings showed that if the person involved was Aboriginal, then the number of offence charges laid did contribute to the referral decision, but this was not true for non-Aborigines. On the other hand, prior Aid Panel appearances were given separate weighting for Aboriginal youth but not for others. It is therefore difficult to avoid the conclusion that Screening Panels take account of somewhat different criteria for each group and, as a result, treat Aborigines differently even from those non-Aborigines who are similar in socio-economic and residential terms.

Nevertheless, since three of the five legal variables tested (the major charge, prior Court appearance records, and the mode of apprehension) are common to the decision-making process for both groups, it is possible that the different legal profiles of these two matched groups help to explain the differentially high rates of Court referrals recorded for Aboriginal youth. To establish this, it must be shown that Aboriginal and non-Aboriginal youth already matched on social background characteristics have an approximately equal probability of being referred to Court if they possess a similar charge profile and offending history. To do this, the logistic regression analysis was extended to produce predictions of the probability of a Court referral. Two sets of tables detailing the predicted probability of a Court referral for every possible 'legal' combination were produced for each group, one dealing with arrest-based appearances only, the other with report-based appearances. By comparing the values generated for the Aboriginal group with the corresponding values produced for the non-Aboriginal group, we can determine whether, for any given combination of legal factors, the two socio-economically matched groups are likely to receive similar treatment from the Screening Panels. If Aborigines consistently record higher probabilities of referral to Court than those non-Aborigines pre-matched on socio-economic criteria, even when the pattern of charging, prior offending histories and methods of apprehension are the same, then this suggests that racial factors influence the operation of discretion at the Screening Panel stage.

For young Aborigines apprehended by means of arrest, the probability of being sent to the Children's Court was generally very high with the single exception of shoplifting (see Appendix 15). In most instances it exceeded 90 chances in 100. Overall, assault recorded the greatest probability of a Court referral, followed by larceny; break, enter, steal; and vehicle theft. Even if they were first offenders, no Aborigines charged with any one of these four crimes had a better than 20 per cent chance of being diverted away from the Children's Court to an Aid Panel. The possession of a prior Aid Panel or Court appearance record simply increased the likelihood of a Court appearance to the point where, in some cases, there was a 100 per cent chance of receiving such an outcome. This applied, for example, to young Aborigines with one or two previous Aid Panel appearances and three or more previous Court appearances who were charged with larceny or break, enter, steal or assault. For arrested non-Aborigines the probabilities of a Court referral were also high, irrespective of the nature of the charge, the number of counts, or prior offending records (see Appendix 16).

More important, however, was the finding that for well over three-quarters (82 per cent, in fact) of all possible combinations of the four legal variables considered, young non-Aborigines had approximately the same chance of being referred to Court as did those Aborigines pre-matched on socio-economic grounds. In other words, in the majority of arrest-based cases, Aboriginal youth is not treated more harshly than is non-Aboriginal youth, once the patterns of charging, prior offending histories and socio-economic factors have been taken into account. This suggests that for young people apprehended by way of arrest, racial factors do not directly exert a consistent influence on the decisions made by Screening Panels.

Nevertheless, racial bias cannot be dismissed from consideration, given the finding that for 18 per cent of all possible 'legal' combinations, the probabilities of a Court referral for the socio-economically matched Aboriginal and non-Aboriginal groups were substantially different, and in the overwhelming majority of these situations, it was Aborigines who were predicted as having the greater chance of being sent to Court. In particular, young Aborigines with no prior Court record charged with only a single offence had a greater likelihood of being referred to Court than did non-Aborigines, and this applied irrespective of the number of previous Aid Panel appearances (see Appendix 17). For example, the probability of a Court referral for a first offender charged with the single offence of break, enter, steal was 84 chances in 100 if he or she was

Aboriginal, but only 59 if non-Aboriginal. If one or two prior Aid Panel appearances are added to this profile, differences in Court referral probabilities became even more pronounced; namely, 98 chances in 100 for Aboriginal youth compared with 59 for non-Aborigines. These results suggest that the absence of a prior Court record has a stronger mitigating effect on 'current' Court referrals if a non-Aboriginal rather than an Aboriginal first offender is involved.

Thus, although racial discrimination does not seem to be a major factor influencing outcomes at a Screening Panel level for arrest-based appearances, a person's racial identity appears to be relevant in certain situations. This finding is important since the non-Aboriginal sample has already been limited to a small number of urban youth who, like city Aborigines, possess poor residential and socio-economic characteristics. It suggests that young Aboriginal offenders are being treated worse even than the very poorest whites. This is a very serious indictment of the system, since for these statistical purposes Aborigines have had to be compared with disadvantaged white youth who themselves are being treated differently from their more prosperous counterparts.

Differences in the treatment of Aborigines and non-Aborigines were even more evident for cases based on a police report. The probability tables (Appendixes 18 and 19) show that for 43 per cent of all possible combinations of the four legal variables considered, Aboriginal and non-Aboriginal youth already matched on socio-economic factors recorded noticeably different probabilities of being referred to Court. And, once again, in the majority of these situations it was the Aborigines who fared the worst, especially in those cases where they had a prior Aid Panel record. Here, young Aborigines were noticeably more likely to come before a Children's Court than were non-Aborigines, and the pattern was particularly pronounced when no prior Court appearances were involved. For example, Aborigines with a record of one or two previous Aid Panel appearances but no prior Court record charged with break, enter, steal had 46 chances in 100 of being referred to Court if reported, compared with 3 in 100 for similarly matched whites. For young people with similar prior records charged with vehicle theft, the chance of a Court referral was 42 in 100 for Aborigines contrasted with only 7 in 100 for non-Aborigines. Thus in appearances based on a police report Aboriginal youth are not always referred in the same way as their matched non-Aboriginal counterparts. These results demonstrate that, little by little, the disadvantage to Aborigines accumulates. Whilst at any one point in the system racial discrimination may not be widespread, the compounding effect of small injustices adds up to a significant difference in overall treatment. And it cannot be overemphasised that this is so even when comparisons are made with whites who are also seriously disadvantaged and inequitably treated by the system.

Nevertheless, these differences between Aborigines and non-Aborigines proved to be less dramatic on the whole than the differences within each group between those cases based on a police report and those brought about by an arrest. The probability of a Court referral for appearances initiated by a police report was consistently lower than that for arrest-based appearances. In the majority of cases the differences were substantial and were evident for both Aborigines and non-Aborigines alike. Thus, for both groups, irrespective of the nature and number of offence charges or prior records, the mode of apprehension was, in most cases, the primary determinant of a Court referral. Screening Panels are far more likely to send arrested individuals to Court than reported ones, irrespective of other legal factors. For example, an Aboriginal with no prior record charged with larceny had 89 chances in 100 of being sent to Court if arrested, but only 15 chances in 100 if reported in the same circumstances. Even Aborigines with prior records are much more likely to be sent to Court if arrested than if reported. For example, an Aboriginal with at least one prior Court and three prior Aid Panel appearances who is charged with disorderly behaviour had a predicted 99 chances in 100 of being sent to Court if arrested but 62 chances in 100 if reported in exactly the same situation.

A comparable pattern of difference emerges when Court referral probabilities for arrested versus reported whites were examined. To take one example, a non-Aboriginal with no prior record and charged with the single offence of larceny faced a probability of a Court referral of only 8 chances in 100 if reported but 79 chances in 100 if arrested. This represents a tenfold increase in the likelihood of being sent to Court by a Screening Panel, and this difference is attributable entirely to being arrested rather than being reported. Thus, in stark contrast to the intent of the legislation, the probability of a Court referral increases substantially when apprehension is based on arrest rather than on a police report. This applies irrespective of the type of offence, the number of offence charges and prior Court records, and it applies to both Aboriginal and non-Aboriginal youth.

These findings squarely contradict a frequently expressed opinion (see, for example, Seymour, 1983: 24) that arrested children go to Court, not because they are arrested but because the police decision to arrest and the Screening Panel decision to send a child to Court are influenced by the same set of external factors. This is simply not true. Even for those Aborigines who have already been matched with non-Aborigines on demographic, residential and socio-economic criteria and further compared to eliminate differences in the type of offence, the number of prior Aid Panel and Court appearances and the number of offence charges, the mode of apprehension remains the prime determinant of a Court referral. The critical result of such decision-making is that substantially more Aboriginal than other young people are sent direct to Court, since proportionately more Aborigines than non-Aborigines are arrested. It is indeed a serious discovery that by using arrest for Aborigines, police are determining the referral decisions made by Screening Panels.

Despite changes to the law in 1979, Screening Panels still direct almost all arrest-based cases to Court. An important legislative change has clearly failed in practice. Moreover these findings demonstrate that decisions taken at one level of the juvenile justice process, namely police apprehension, have a significant impact at the second level, namely Court referral.

These results cast serious doubt upon the objectivity and independence of the Screening Panel as a pre-trial mechanism. Arrest is not even mentioned in Screening Panel guidelines as a criterion relevant to the decision to refer a case to Court. Why then does it assume such importance in practice? We can only speculate, since Screening Panel deliberations are inaccessible to observers. However, one reason may lie in the composition of the Screening Panel itself, consisting as it does of one police officer and one community welfare worker. Informal discussions with police officers have revealed that the police representative on the Screening Panel is often placed under considerable pressure by fellow officers to ensure that an arrested person is brought before the Court. Having made an arrest and completed all the paperwork associated with it, the apprehending officers want their action validated by a Court appearance, which at least entails the formal laying of charges and the likelihood that the individual will receive some sort of punishment and acquire a criminal record. This contrasts with the totally non-punitive approach of Aid Panels.

Some Community Welfare workers who sat on Screening Panels indicated that the police member tended to dominate the screenings, and recalled instances where the latter had actually arrived at the Panel meeting with the recommendation for a Court appearance already filled in on the referral form. Some of the welfare workers were relatively young and inexperienced and found it difficult to 'stand up' to the police representative, who in most cases was a senior officer with considerable experience. The circumstances under which Screening Panels met to consider arrests often increased the social worker's disadvantage. Under the terms of the legislation, all arrested cases must be brought before the Children's Court within one full working day of the arrest. As a result, screenings are often carried out at extremely short notice and are subject to severe time restrictions. As one Community Welfare worker commented, when faced with twenty screenings on a Saturday morning, there was a tendency to give no more consideration to outcomes than would be involved if a coin was tossed. The tossing of a coin, however, would probably be fairer than the outcomes observed here.

It is interesting to note that, in the event of unresolvable disagreement between the two Screening Panel members, the legislation allows for the case to be forwarded to a judge or magistrate of the Children's Court for adjudication. Yet over a seven-year period, during which some 60,000 cases were screened, only a handful required such adjudication by an independent third party. Such a high level of agreement between two representatives who traditionally hold radically different views on the treatment of young offenders is, to say the least, surprising.

Summary

This chapter has demonstrated that in certain circumstances, Screening Panels operate in a manner which disadvantages Aboriginal youth even in comparison with white youth from similarly poor socio-economic circumstances. When those Aboriginal appearances which took place in Adelaide during one year were matched with an equal number of non-Aboriginal appearances on the basis of age, sex, occupation, family structure and residential location, it was found that young Aborigines were still significantly more likely than other young people to be referred to Court rather than diverted to an Aid Panel. When logistic regression analysis was subsequently applied to these Aboriginal appearances and (separately) to the pre-matched non-Aboriginal appearances in order to test the relevance to the referral decision of certain legal factors, it was found that a different set of legal criteria contributed to that decision, depending on whether the offender was Aboriginal or not.

Moreover, even when the two groups possessed the same legal profiles as well as social background characteristics, some differences in Court referral were still present. More specifically, it was the Aborigines who were generally more likely to be denied the opportunity of diversion to an Aid Panel. It would appear that only the operation of some degree of racial bias could account for these inconsistent applications.

Even more significant, however, is the indisputable fact that the disadvantage young Aborigines suffer by being arrested in such large numbers is compounded at the Screening Panel level. The introduction of Panels as pre-trial filters was designed to benefit young people by ensuring greater equity for those who were socially disadvantaged. Yet they do not appear to have achieved their legislative goal. In fact, they do the reverse. Disadvantage is heaped upon disadvantage, casting serious doubt upon the whole concept of justice.

These results clearly support Feeley's (1979) argument that to concentrate solely on the final stages of Court adjudication and disposition in the criminal process gives a distorted and incomplete picture of the real impact of that process on an accused. Whilst it is important to investigate Aboriginal rates of detention, it is equally if not more important to examine the operation of the various pre-trial mechanisms, since these affect a far greater number of accused young people. As evidenced here, young Aborigines have already experienced considerable disadvantage long before they even reach the final stages of disposition. The mere fact that so many end up in Court is in itself an indictment of the system and its inability to deliver justice equitably to all young persons. The process of differential treatment begins much earlier, at the very first point of contact with police. From the first encounter, through the charging process and arrest, to pre-trial filtering and eventually to Court, Aborigines are given the more serious outcomes of the options available to decision-makers. In so doing, little by little their relative situation deteriorates and nowhere can this be demonstrated more clearly than at the pre-trial stage, which in South Australia means a Screening Panel. The very structure that was intended to give greater opportunity to the disadvantaged and to keep young people out of the formal processing mechanisms has failed to achieve its goal.

7

Panels and Courts:
What is Resolved?

For a young accused person in South Australia, the final stage in the criminal justice process is either an appearance before a Children's Aid Panel or formal prosecution in the Children's Court. This chapter examines whether Aborigines suffer any disadvantage in either situation.

In doing so, it should be stressed that disadvantage to Aborigines has already occurred long before the dispositional stage is reached. The evidence for this lies in the disproportionately low numbers of Aboriginal children who are referred to Children's Aid Panels. This has important consequences for young Aborigines, because Aid Panel and Court appearances are wholly different in nature and outcome. An appearance before an Aid Panel is at once less stigmatising and more constructive, and does not involve the delays which may be attendant upon the processes which make up a Children's Court hearing. Thus a child who is sent to an Aid Panel will leave the criminal process at an earlier and lower stage than his or her counterpart who is sent to Court. By channelling such a disproportionate number of Aboriginal youth into the formal Court system, Screening Panels are effectively depriving them of the opportunity to benefit from the constructive intervention which diversion offers. To deny equitable access to this benefit is to deny social justice. By contrast, a Court appearance ensures that young Aborigines will be processed to the full extent of the law. Not only does it increase the likelihood that they will leave the system with a criminal record which they will carry into their adult lives, but it means that they must also endure the full effects of the Court's pre-adjudication process which has been correctly identified by Feeley (1979) as a punishment in its own right.

Specific Court practices, such as the use of adjournments, transference of cases from one Court to another and obtaining legal representation, must all be considered in the context of the thesis that the 'process is the punishment'. If Aborigines are being sentenced differently from their white counterparts, this will merely be the culmination of differential treatment shown to exist at every stage of the juvenile justice system.

Diversion: Children's Aid Panels

The rationale underlying the establishment of a diversion system is that it is neither necessary nor desirable for all offenders to appear in Court. The argument for diversion is supported by labelling theory, which can be summed up as 'give a dog a bad name': a Court appearance stigmatises the child who will subsequently regard himself or herself as a criminal and act accordingly. More positively, it can be argued that informal procedures provide the opportunity for dealing with a child's behavioural problems more constructively than does a Court appearance, and this reduces the likelihood of further offending. In addition, there are economic justifications for the diversion of appropriate cases: non-serious matters do not warrant the time and expense of a full Court hearing. Hence, diversionary procedures, wherever they exist, usually aim to keep non-serious matters and first offenders out of Court. This is the role played by Children's Aid Panels.

South Australia has adopted the model of a professionally constituted diversionary body; thus Aid Panels consist of a representative from each of the two government departments most closely involved with young offenders, namely the police and Community Welfare. The commitment to professional composition means that in truancy or drug matters there is also a representative from the education or health department. This model is also adhered to in Western Australia. The contrary argument is that the function of Panels is best discharged by representatives from the general community. Thus Children's Hearings in Scotland (Martin and Murray, 1982) consist of three lay members who

> have no connection with the system of criminal justice . . . They are members of the public who have offered themselves for unpaid service in the Children's Hearing system and have been selected as suitable for the task (McCabe and Treitel, 1983: 33ff).

One of the assumed advantages of Children's Aid Panel appearances is their relative informality: thus the stigmatising effect of a Court hearing is avoided. Hence, Aid Panels in South Australia sit in Community Welfare offices and not in police stations. Whilst a child must be given proper notice of the sitting and of the allegations in order to conform with the demands of due process so strongly emphasised in *Re Gault* (1967: U.S. 1), the Aid Panel's procedure is informal. No legal representation is permitted, although the child and others may, at the Aid Panel's discretion, make submissions. The sitting usually lasts no more than forty-five minutes and the young person attends together with one or both parents.

Since Children's Aid Panels are not Courts and cannot pronounce on guilt or innocence, it is a precondition of a case being dealt with in this less formal way that the child admit the allegation. The same precondition exists in the Western Australian system. There is a strongly held view that diversionary procedures will have a constructive effect on an offender only if that person voluntarily co-operates and acknowledges responsibility. On the other hand this precondition could be viewed as introducing an undesirable element of disguised coercion, inducing children to 'admit' to offences they did not in reality commit.

Given that disproportionately few young Aborigines are referred to Children's Aid Panels in the first place, it is interesting that the cases which actually reach them do not reveal any differences in outcome when compared with those of non-Aboriginal children. Once Aboriginal cases are actually diverted into the Children's Aid Panel system, the statistics reveal no evidence of discriminatory treatment. The overwhelming majority of all appearances before Aid Panels result in the child being warned and counselled, and this is true whether she or he is Aboriginal or not. Over the five-year study period, very few appearances resulted in an undertaking by the child (6.8 per cent for Aborigines and 5.3 per cent for others) and virtually no parents were required to enter into an undertaking. Thus Aid Panels do not treat Aboriginal children differently from other young people. Indeed their limited powers would make differential treatment virtually impossible.

The real issue at stake, then, is that so few Aboriginal children are given the opportunity of diversion. Reasons frequently cited to account for the low rate of Aid Panel referrals for Aboriginal youth include failure to attend the hearing, failure of a parent to accompany the child and the child's likelihood of breaching any undertaking given to the Panel. Yet these arguments are not supported by the evidence. In reality, the overwhelming majority of Aboriginal children sent to Aid Panels (93.1 per cent of 949 cases studied) did in fact appear with a parent and had their cases successfully completed. Only 4.2 per cent had to be referred on by Aid Panels to the Children's Court for failure to attend the Panel hearing, and in only 0.5 per cent of cases did the child fail to comply with or subsequently breach an undertaking. This proportion was the same as that recorded for non-Aborigines. Hence the view that young Aborigines are less suitable candidates for the diversionary process is certainly not borne out by the outcomes for those who are referred to Panels.

Clearly then, the principal defect of the diversionary system of Children's Aid Panels for young Aborigines is that many of them are denied access to it. Whatever criticisms may be levelled against Aid Panels, from a young person's perspective they are unarguably a preferable route to the formality of a Court appearance. From society's point of view, they offer an early chance of crime prevention. For these reasons alone the fact that low numbers of Aboriginal children are referred to them is a denial of social justice, particularly since the referral pattern cannot be explained simply in terms of types of offences or past records of offenders. Moreover, since there is little difference in Aid Panel outcomes for

Aboriginal and other children, it could be argued that greater diversion for Aborigines would ensure greater equity in the delivery of justice to this minority group.

Disposition: The Children's Court

The Children's Court procedure, in the exercise of its criminal jurisdiction, is essentially that of a Magistrates' Court with appropriate modifications. Proceedings are initiated by the police and legal representation is permitted. In the interests of the child, the Court is a closed court and statute restricts the publication of details identifying an accused. The Court retains a significant social welfare input at the dispositional stage, where the judicial officer takes account of reports presented by the Department for Community Welfare. This provides a clear illustration of a mixed model of juvenile justice, based on concepts of both welfare and justice.

The Adelaide Children's Court has specially designated judges and magistrates who sit full-time, but elsewhere, particularly in country areas, no comparable degree of specialisation exists: magistrates combine Children's Court work with their general jurisdiction. The absence of a specialised judiciary in large parts of Australia is unavoidable for geographical reasons. Yet this may have implications for the outcome of the Court process, principally in relation to sentencing. Both the jurisdiction and sentencing powers of magistrates are restricted by statute. It can also be argued that judicial officers who do not specialise in cases involving young offenders have a different attitude towards sentencing and that their sentencing pattern differs from that of their specialist colleagues.

As already shown in Chapter 2, the sentencing policy applied by the Children's Court is quite different from that applied by courts sentencing adults. The primary emphasis is on rehabilitation of the individual child; the Court's order is tailored to this aim. The powers of the Court, once a young person has been found guilty of committing an offence, are wide. The most serious penalty is detention for two months to two years, though the maximum can be imposed only by a judge. The period of detention is now fixed by the Court itself and not, as under the repealed legislation, left to the discretion of the Minister of Community Welfare (who was the child's guardian). Thus the line of demarcation between the roles of criminal justice and of welfare intervention is now clear-cut. A young offender does not serve a sentence in an ordinary prison but in a Training Centre — a special institution for those under eighteen years of age run by the Department for Community Welfare.

In recent years there has been a trend away from actual detention of young persons, and South Australia is no exception. Under the current legislation the Children's Court may suspend a sentence of detention and place the young offender on a bond subject to conditions, one of which may be community service.

Placing a child on a bond for up to two years is an important part of the Children's Court's powers. A bond is essentially a contract between the Court and the child. Various conditions may be written into the terms; the Court has wide discretion to 'tailor' the bond to fit the rehabilitation needs of a particular child. For example, it may be a condition of the bond that the child be supervised by a social worker. The Court also has the power to fine, although this will be a practicable option only where the offender's resources permit. Consistent with the trend away from actual detention, a child who defaults on a fine may carry out community work to discharge the debt. Finally, the Court is able to discharge a child without penalty. If a child appears in Court on multiple charges, only one penalty is usually imposed, although that may take account of all charges. Fines and bonds may be imposed simultaneously.

The Children's Court of South Australia does not have to record a conviction except when a sentence of detention is involved.

Aborigines Before the Children's Court

That disproportionate numbers of blacks throughout the Western world are imprisoned is well known and well publicised, and young Aboriginal offenders in South Australia prove to be no exception. At the point of sentencing by the Children's Court, their detention rate is some twenty-three times greater than expected given their population numbers. But other startling patterns emerge at the final disposition stage. There is clear evidence that the force of decisions taken at the early levels of the criminal justice process permeates the whole system, including the orders awarded by the Court.

Moreover, because the ideals of juvenile justice, in providing rehabilitation for the individual, necessitate the consideration of socio-economic factors at the point of sentencing, those individuals from backgrounds not conforming to the norms of white middle-class society are selected for a different degree of State intervention than their more socially 'fortunate' counterparts. As a result, although it is not possible to identify racial bias as such operating in the Children's Court, nevertheless the pre-existing social and economic disadvantage of young Aborigines is compounded by the operation of a well-meaning and well-intentioned system which is designed to lead to their rehabilitation.

Irrespective of the outcome, the adjudication process itself is a significant experience for the young people. In fact, because a substantial proportion of young persons appearing in Court were eventually discharged without penalty or conviction, it was often the Court process itself rather than the outcome which entailed the greatest punishment. This was particularly true for young Aborigines. Consequently, in order to obtain an overall picture of Court procedures as they operate for Aborigines and other young people, the ensuing discussion not only considers the sentencing decision itself but also focuses on a number of different aspects of that Court process, including the extent of legal representation, the nature of pleas and the frequency of adjournments.

Nature of the Pleas Entered

The Children's Court is essentially intended to operate as an adversarial system, with proceedings being initiated by police and contested by the accused with the assistance, if sought, of legal representation. Yet in reality, the primary role of the Court is one of disposition rather than adjudication. The reason for this is the overwhelming number of guilty pleas. The majority who come before the Children's Court admit the allegation; this applies to Aborigines and non-Aborigines alike. During the five-year study period, 99.6 per cent and 99.5 per cent of Aboriginal and non-Aboriginal appearances respectively involved a plea of guilty.

Why do so many young people plead guilty? The proposition that police operate with total accuracy, apprehending only those who are actually responsible for committing crimes, has been refuted by Aboriginal workers and legal representatives. Instead, it seems that certain hidden forces are at work, encouraging this acquiescent response. One possibility is that, because an appearance before an Aid Panel requires an admission of the allegation, this unwittingly carries over into the Court process. Probably a more important factor, especially amongst Aboriginal youth, is the desire to have the matter disposed of quickly. The general (but not always accurate) belief is that if they plead guilty to a charge, the case will be processed more swiftly. A not-guilty plea inevitably results in a trial which may take months before it is scheduled for hearing. Moreover, the trial itself may run over a number of consecutive days, with the child being required to attend Court on each of those days. For many young people, this in itself is a daunting prospect, which is further accentuated by the ordeal of giving evidence and facing cross-examination by the police prosecutor.

Pre-trial negotiations also play an important role, albeit one that is difficult to monitor. According to a directive issued by the senior judge of the Children's Court, when a young person indicates his or her intention to contest a charge, negotiations between the child's lawyer and the police prosecutor must take place before the matter comes to trial. Such negotiations not infrequently result in an offer from the prosecutor to substitute less serious charges in exchange for a plea of guilty. If the accused refuses the offer and proceeds with the trial, he or she runs the risk of losing the case. If, on the other hand, he or she pleads guilty to the lesser charges, a more lenient penalty may result. To increase the pressure placed on the child, such offers are sometimes withheld until just moments before the trial is scheduled to commence. In one instance, a young Aboriginal spent almost sixty days in custody awaiting trial. Barely two minutes before the hearing was to begin, the police prosecutor offered to negotiate. The lawyer had very little time to explain the new developments to the boy and make him aware of their implications, while for his part, the young person, already intimidated and confused by the unfamiliarity of the Court setting and fearful of the pending trial, was not in a position to make a considered, informed judgement. His decision to accept the prosecutor's offer by pleading guilty to less serious charges was, in the circumstances, not surprising. Such practices imply a strong element of coercion in the justice process, and indicate that the rights implicit in the traditional model of due process are not, in practice, being accorded children.

For the relatively few young people who persist with their claim of innocence and do have 'their day in Court', the experience can prove to be so traumatic that it effectively deters them from pursuing a similar course on future occasions. In one of the relatively few instances observed in which a young Aboriginal pleaded not guilty to charges of resisting arrest and assaulting police, the trial lasted for three days, at the end of which the boy and his family were physically and emotionally exhausted. The young accused obviously lacked sufficient verbal skills to present his evidence in a cogent fashion and quickly became confused when subjected to intense and hostile questioning by the prosecutor. Aboriginal witnesses, who supported his version of events, suffered a similar fate. He was subsequently found guilty and convicted. Some months later this same young man was again arrested and charged with disorderly behaviour and resisting arrest. He was adamant that he was innocent of the charges, but opted to plead guilty to avoid the trauma of another trial and what he saw as an inevitable verdict of guilty at the end of it.

The overwhelming tendency to admit guilt means that for most young people, a Children's Court appearance results in a criminal record. Although many believe that their juvenile records are destroyed once they turn eighteen, this is not the case. If they offend as adults, all details of their Children's Court appearances in which guilt was established are forwarded to the adult Court and are taken into account during sentencing. It is not unusual, then, for Aborigines to be sentenced to imprisonment at their first adult appearance for a relatively minor offence primarily because of their long record of Children's Court appearances. Once again, this highlights the serious implications of the Screening Panel's decision to refer such a disproportionate number of young Aborigines to Court. By so doing, they are virtually guaranteeing a criminal record for the majority of Aborigines who pass through the juvenile justice system. Diversion to an Aid Panel for the majority of non-Aboriginal offenders prevents many in this group from experiencing a similar fate.

Legal Representation

The impact of legal representation must be considered against the background that the Children's Court is primarily concerned with disposition rather than adjudication. Legal representation proved to be an exception to the general finding that Aborigines are disadvantaged within the juvenile justice system. During the five-year period of study, a significantly greater proportion of Aboriginal than non-Aboriginal cases were legally represented: 71.2 per cent compared with 47.7 per cent respectively. These differences were evident not only in Adelaide but also in rural and remote areas of the State. In fact, the largest disparity in legal representation occurred in remote South Australia, where over three-quarters of all Aboriginal appearances had a lawyer present, compared with only 29.7 per cent of all non-Aboriginal appearances.

The explanation for these different rates of representation between Aboriginal and non-Aboriginal youth lies in the ready availability of legal aid for Aborigines. In South Australia, the Aboriginal Legal Rights Movement first began operations in 1971. It employs one lawyer on a full-time basis to handle all cases coming before the Adelaide Children's Court. Other Legal Rights lawyers, although not specialising solely in children's matters, provide representation for Aboriginal young offenders appearing before the suburban Courts. Separate Legal Rights Offices, staffed by at least one lawyer and a field officer, are located in key country centres. Consequently, most areas of the State where sizeable Aboriginal communities are located are serviced by the Movement. In rural communities where direct access to a Legal Rights lawyer is lacking, such as those in the south-east of the State, cases are briefed out by the Movement to private legal practitioners. The end result is that, whereas Aborigines are disadvantaged generally in relation to the criminal justice system, in the provision of legal aid they appear to be advantaged.

Since the overwhelming majority of children who appear in the Children's Court eventually plead guilty, what is the role of such legal representation? Lawyers who represent young people in Court see their main function as one of protecting the legal rights of the young person, in particular by ensuring that the plea entered is an appropriate one. If necessary, the lawyer will, on the child's behalf, negotiate with the police prosecution in an attempt to secure the elimination of certain charges or the substitution of less serious charges. This is of obvious benefit to the child if it results in a less serious penalty. At the Court hearing itself, the lawyer operates as an intermediary who protects and supports the accused during what may be a traumatic experience. If a lawyer is present, the judge or magistrate normally directs his or her remarks to that lawyer, rather than to the child: a practice which removes at least some of the pressure from the young accused. The lawyer is also able to interpret the often confusing process of a Court hearing and ensure that the child understands the outcomes of the appearance. Yet, despite these obvious benefits, lawyers may be a mixed blessing. It seems that they are at least partly responsible for the disproportionately high levels of adjournments experienced by Aboriginal youth. Moreover, they do not seem to exert much influence at the dispositional stage of the hearing, although this is an area which is difficult to assess because of the complexity of the sentencing process. A 'tariff' system of penalties is inappropriate in the juvenile context (see Chapter 2). Instead, the sentencing process is highly individualised, the order being tailored to effect the rehabilitation of the young person. Wide discretion is vested in the judicial officer presiding. The Court not only receives submissions from the young person's lawyer but also seeks a social work perspective: thus the Department for Community Welfare is invited to submit reports, including recommendations on an appropriate order. There is, therefore, no simple relationship between the existence of legal representation and the outcome of the Court process. Perhaps it is not surprising then that, at the point of sentencing, Aborigines do not seem to fare better than their non-Aboriginal counterparts, even though almost twice as many of them are legally represented.

Social Background and Assessment Panel Reports

Two types of report may be requested by the Children's Court to assist in the determination of an appropriate order. Social Background Reports are relatively common, while the more rigorous Assessment Panel Reports are utilised primarily in cases where detention or attendance at a project centre is contemplated. Both types of reports are requested more frequently in Aboriginal cases than in others. During the five-year survey period, Social Background Reports were submitted in 47 per cent of all Aboriginal compared with 39 per cent of all non-Aboriginal cases. The figures for Assessment Panel Reports were 29 per cent and 18 per cent respectively.

These reports ensure input by social workers into the sentencing process. They contain details of previous Court or Aid Panel appearances, as well as personal particulars on the child, his or her parents and other members of the family. Educational and occupational details are recorded, with particular stress placed on attitudinal aspects, such as punctuality and enthusiasm for work or school. Other areas include participation in sporting activities, relationships with friends and family members, and 'home management', which notes the type of house occupied by the family, their financial situation and subjective comments regarding the neatness and cleanliness of the house.

Commonly, the reports contain specific recommendations on appropriate penalties. Although the Court is in no way bound to follow them, it often does. To cite just one of many examples, in the case of a seventeen-year-old Aboriginal male, the report recommended a fine. In addition, it suggested that he be placed on a six-month bond with supervision and to attend programs and projects as directed. In this, as in many other cases, the presiding judge adopted these sentencing recommendations in full.

The on-going use of such reports in the criminal jurisdiction of the Children's Court is not without its critics. Some feel that the welfare component in sentencing is too great and that the appropriate penalty is not, in practice, the decision of the judge or magistrate, but in many cases that of the officers of the Department for Community Welfare. The use of these reports at the sentencing stage has particular ramifications for young Aborigines. The inclusion in such reports of details on factors such as home environment, gives free rein to the expression of white middle-class values which are not necessarily appropriate in a differing cultural context.

A more concrete criticism is the delays which the preparation of reports often entail. This occurs particularly in the case of children who have been arrested: such cases must come before the Children's Court within one full working day of the arrest. Obviously this leaves little time for the preparation of a detailed Social Background Report and so the normal procedure is for the matter to be adjourned pending the preparation of the report. Such delays can become quite lengthy, as the following example illustrates. An Aboriginal male was arrested in Adelaide and charged with assaulting police. After entering a plea of guilty, the matter was adjourned for some four weeks to allow for the preparation of a Social Background Report. When the boy appeared in Court at the appointed time, fully expecting, as did his lawyer, that the outstanding matters would be dealt with, the Court was informed that the Social Background Report was not ready. A further adjournment was ordered, but at the rescheduled hearing some four weeks later, the Court was informed that, although the Social Background Report had been completed, it was in a taxi in transit to the Court from the local Community Welfare office. In view of its non-arrival, the Court had no option but to order yet another adjournment. By the time the matter was finally dealt with, some three months had elapsed. Yet, although the boy had privately maintained that he was innocent of the charges, he had opted to plead guilty in the expectation that this would lead to a speedy resolution of his case. Such delays in the production of Social Background Reports potentially affect more Aboriginal than non-Aboriginal children for two reasons: firstly, reports are requested more frequently in Aboriginal cases, and secondly, more young Aborigines appear by way of arrest, thereby increasing the chances that an adjournment will be needed to secure the report's preparation. The latter situation illustrates yet again how a decision taken at one level of the criminal justice process can unwittingly affect the operation of that process at subsequent levels.

The Use of Adjournments

Delays in the criminal justice process can operate at great cost to the accused individual. In theory, delays should affect all racial groups equally, but in reality the internal workings of the juvenile justice process have more impact on young Aborigines than on their non-Aboriginal counterparts.

An often overlooked consequence of the Screening Panel's decision to direct the majority of Aboriginal cases to the Children's Court rather than diverting them to Aid Panels is the disproportionately large number of adjournments experienced by Aborigines, simply because these occur far more commonly in the Court process than in the Aid Panel system. In fact, of the 22,080 adjournments recorded during the five-year period, only 1.4 per cent were ordered by Aid Panels. Moreover, once in Court, a higher proportion of Aboriginal than other cases were adjourned, and adjourned more often. Of the 2361 Aboriginal Court cases, 67.3 per cent were adjourned at least once, 44.6 per cent recorded two or more adjournments, while 9.2 per cent involved five or more adjournments. Corresponding figures for non-Aboriginal Court appearances were consistently lower: 53.7 per cent, 30.1 per cent and 5.0 per cent respectively.

This pattern exists irrespective of the type of adjournment involved. To illustrate, 22.4 per cent of all Aboriginal Court appearances involved at least one simple adjournment which imposed no conditions or constraints upon the individual, contrasted with only 6.2 per cent of all non-Aboriginal appearances. Almost one-half (42.7 per cent) of all Aboriginal appearances involved at least one bail adjournment, compared with only 38.6 per cent of non-Aboriginal appearances. Finally, 25.5 per cent of all Aboriginal appearances, compared with only 11.5 per cent of all non-Aboriginal appearances, involved at least one custody adjournment.

Disturbingly, Aboriginal over-representation is most pronounced in relation to the most serious type of adjournment: those where the accused child is held in custody. Although Aboriginal youth accounted for 16.8 per cent of all Court appearances which had at least one adjournment, they made up 26.3 per cent of those appearances involving a custody adjournment but only 15.1 per cent of appearances involving a bail adjournment. The maximum duration for a custody order is twenty-eight days and since a number of such adjournments may be required in a particular case, some youths end up spending a substantial period in custody before their cases are finalised. There is no clearer example of the real cost to the individual of the pre-sentence process.

The positive benefits of the adjournment process are often stressed by Court personnel. If legal representation has not been obtained, the Court often adjourns the matter to give the child the opportunity to consult a lawyer. In turn, the lawyer may request more time to obtain a full briefing from his or her client. Such requests are often made by lawyers representing Aborigines. The extremely limited resources available to the Legal Rights Movement means that these lawyers usually work under considerable pressure and often simply do not have time to prepare for a case unless an adjournment is granted. Further delays occur when not-guilty pleas are indicated. These are required to enable the police and defence counsel to negotiate issues of common ground. As previously stated, adjournments are also ordered to allow time for the preparation of Social Background and other reports.

Yet all the positive benefits of adjournment must be weighed against the real cost of delays to the individual, especially if these delays result in a deprivation of liberty. Young Aborigines whom we interviewed frequently did not comprehend the reason for many delays, especially when they intended to enter a plea of guilty. At times, these delays became quite ludicrous. To cite just one example: an Aboriginal youth was arrested on two charges: illegal use of a motor vehicle and driving without a licence. The first appearance before a suburban Court (A) was adjourned to enable the boy to seek legal advice. At the second appearance some two weeks later, legal assistance had not been obtained so another adjournment was ordered. The same fate befell the third and fourth appearances. At the fifth appearance, he had obtained the assistance of a lawyer, but because he now had matters outstanding before another Court (B), the magistrate decided to adjourn so that all offence charges could be consolidated into the one hearing before Court B. However, when the boy and his lawyer appeared at that Court some weeks later, it was found that the relevant files had not been transferred. The case was adjourned until the next day where an appearance was scheduled back at Court A. Again, the youth and his lawyer appeared but the person presiding at Court A decided that his original decision to transfer the case to Court B still had merit, and acted accordingly. Some two weeks later, at Court B, the eighth appearance took place. This time some progress was made: the boy entered a plea of guilty. At this point, the magistrate adjourned proceedings so that a Social Background Report could be prepared. Two more adjournments were required, however, before the report was submitted to the Court. It was not until the eleventh appearance, which took place some seven months after the initial hearing, that the matter was finally resolved. The end result? Both charges were dismissed without penalty, with no conviction being recorded. In terms of the final outcome, the boy was not subjected to any form of punishment. Yet this obscures the fact that, in the process, he had to endure eleven Court appearances, with all the attendant stress: stress which in this case was heightened by his knowledge that, because he had originally been arrested and bailed, failure to appear on any one of the eleven occasions would have meant the loss of his bail money, possibly followed by his arrest and detention. Because his case was shuffled between two Courts, his travelling commitments were extensive, as was the time missed from school. Finally, the costs to the lawyer and to the Court system itself must have been considerable. This is a clear illustration of Feeley's argument that the process itself may be the greatest punishment. This is particularly ironic here, where the process is intended to work to the advantage of youth: hence the five adjournments ordered so that he could obtain legal advice, and the three adjournments for a Social Background Report. Even the decision to transfer the case to another Court was done in the best interests of the boy: namely, to allow all of his outstanding charges to be dealt with together, thereby avoiding overlapping appearances for different matters. The end result of these good intentions, however, was to trap him in the system for a considerable period of time. Nor was this case unusual.

The adjournment process can therefore generate negative consequences and contribute to the real costs of the Court experience for the individual concerned. It can also lead to its own form of 'offending' and punishment. For example, a young Aboriginal male, aged fifteen years, was released on bail when his case was adjourned pending the preparation of a Social Background Report. He was notified of the date and time of the next appearance, but he failed to appear. A warrant was issued, he was arrested and spent several days in detention for non-appearance in Court. When released, he still faced another Court appearance to deal with the original list of offences. The punishment he received for failing to appear in Court was, in fact, far more severe than the penalty imposed for the offending behaviour which brought him into the system in the first place. Once again, this illustrates that the real impact of the criminal justice process is not adequately gauged by a concentration only on the ultimate stage of sentencing. Real costs have often been experienced far earlier.

The Judicial Officer Presiding

Yet another area where significant differences emerge between Aborigines and other young people is in the proportion of appearances which are heard by specialised, full-time judges of the Children's Court and those which are dealt with by magistrates. In fact, Children's Court judges presided over 37.3 per cent of all Aboriginal cases while 59.7 per cent went before a magistrate. By contrast, non-Aboriginal cases were fairly evenly divided between the two: 49.6 per cent were dealt with by a judge, 49.7 per cent by a magistrate. (Very few cases of either group take place before a justice of the peace because of the limited role played by such personnel in the juvenile system.)

These differences have clear implications for sentencing. Because the judges deal exclusively with children's matters, they are totally familiar with the Court's procedures and the legislative requirements pertaining to children, in particular the need to achieve a balance at the disposition stage between the rehabilitation of the child and the protection of the community. By contrast, most magistrates, especially those working in rural areas, usually combine Children's Court with general work. They are therefore required to operate within two distinctly different jurisdictions: that is, in the adult system, where general deterrence and proportionality between crime and punishment assume significance, and the juvenile system with its emphasis on the welfare and rehabilitation of the individual. Interviews with various Court personnel indicate that the transition from one to the other is not always achieved, with magistrates accustomed to the adult jurisdiction at times applying harsher adult sentencing principles to Children's Court matters, while failing to give adequate weight to welfare considerations. Lawyers also claim that non-specialised magistrates, because they are less practised in Children's Court work, tend to be less consistent in the orders they impose and the hearings themselves tend to be more confused and disjointed. In contrast, the sentencing practices of the Adelaide's Children's Court judges are considered to be highly consistent and predictable, and the whole Court process operates far more smoothly and with greater efficiency. Clearly, then, the fact that proportionately more Aboriginal than non-Aboriginal youth comes before a magistrate may have important ramifications. Yet this is not an intentional decision to disadvantage Aboriginal youth; the differences are readily explained in terms of geographic location. The majority of apprehended Aboriginal youth resides in rural areas where the Children's Court jurisdiction is not specialised and hearings are invariably conducted by magistrates. It is solely their predominantly rural location which places more Aboriginal than non-Aboriginal youth before a magistrate.

Nevertheless, some young people from rural or remote areas of the State do have their cases transferred to the city. This applied to some 18.7 per cent of those appearances involving rural-based Aboriginal youth and 19.9 per cent of appearances by Aboriginal youth living in the remote North-West and West of South Australia. Corresponding transfer figures for non-Aboriginal appearances by rural and remote-dwelling youth were somewhat lower; namely, 12.9 per cent and 15.6 per cent respectively. This practice of transferring cases to Adelaide may have serious consequences for young Aborigines, especially those from the traditionally-based communities in the North-West of the State. Such young people may be sent to the city to avoid delays in judicial processing arising from the fact that a Children's Court is convened only once every several months in the more remote areas such as the Pitjantjatjara lands. Young women and men transferred to Adelaide are normally held in custody pending their Court appearance — an experience which is often alienating and frightening. In addition, critics of this practice argue that it brings them into contact with relatively experienced urban-based offenders, from whom they learn such skills as how to steal a car, how to break and enter, etc.

Penalties

Statistical analysis of the sentencing process of the Children's Court is problematical, since the penalty is tailored to the perceived needs of the individual child. In addition to the 'welfare' input of Social Background and Assessment Panel Reports at the dispositional stage, the child may have appeared on multiple charges and so an order may reflect other offences in respect of which he or she was formally discharged. The data analysed here consider only the penalty imposed for what was coded as the major charge. This analysis therefore assumes a direct relationship between the major charge and the major charge penalty.

Notwithstanding these provisos, when the sentencing stage of the Children's Court process is finally reached, Aborigines still appear to be treated differently from other youth. Yet the pattern of differential treatment is somewhat unexpected. In general terms, Aboriginal appearances are more likely to result in a detention or suspended detention order, a supervised bond or a discharge than are non-Aboriginal appearances. They are far less likely to be given a fine or an unsupervised bond. Thus they appear in disproportionately high numbers at both the top and bottom ends of the penalty scale. These patterns are summarised in Table 7.1.

(a) Detention

A sentence of detention represents the most severe penalty which can be imposed by the Children's Court. It is, as Table 7.1 indicates, a relatively uncommon outcome of Court proceedings for both Aborigines and non-Aborigines, with judges and magistrates using it only as a 'last resort'. Nevertheless, a higher proportion of Aboriginal than non-Aboriginal appearances have this outcome. Detention, both actual and suspended, accounted for 10.3 per cent of all Aboriginal appearances, but only 4.2 per cent of appearances by other young people. Moreover, Aboriginal children have not apparently benefited as much as their non-Aboriginal counterparts from recent policy moves which favour alternatives to actual detention — for instance, suspended sentences with bond conditions, one of which now may be community service. In fact, only 47.5 per cent of detention sentences for Aborigines were suspended compared with 57.1 per cent for non-Aborigines.

Table 7.1: Penalties imposed for the major charge in all Aboriginal and non-Aboriginal appearances before the Children's Court

Penalty	Aborigines %	Non-Aborigines %
Detention	5.4	1.8
Detention — suspended	4.9	2.4
Bond*	7.9	14.2
Bond with supervision	23.2	15.8
Bond — other†	2.2	3.0
Fine	24.7	36.1
Discharge	31.7	26.7
Total	100.0	100.0
	n=2358‡	n=14626‡

*This refers to a simple bond of good behaviour with no additional conditions attached.

†This refers to a bond in combination with a fine, or attendance at a youth project centre or community work.

‡These figures exclude 3 Aboriginal and 38 non-Aboriginal appearances involving committal for trial in an adult court.

(b) Bonds

In the middle-order of the penalty range, namely bonds, no pattern of differential treatment is immediately discernible: bonds were ordered in 33.2 per cent of Aboriginal appearances and 33.0 per cent of other appearances. Yet on closer analysis, differences did emerge. Aboriginal appearances more commonly result in a bond with supervision than do non-Aboriginal appearances, whereas the reverse is true of simple, unsupervised bonds. A bond with supervision obviously represents a greater degree of intervention than does an unsupervised bond.

Aboriginal welfare workers have voiced criticism of the use of both supervised and unsupervised bonds by the Children's Court. One complaint is that a lengthy bond imposed for a relatively minor offence is a response to the child's family problems rather than to the offence itself. In effect, it permits a degree of welfare intervention which is not in keeping with the non-serious nature of the child's offending behaviour. Bonds may also be inappropriate for traditionally oriented children living in remote areas; bond conditions may simply not be culturally relevant to such children and supervision poses very real practical problems in many rural as well as remote areas.

(c) Fines

As would be expected given their economic circumstances, proportionately fewer Aboriginal appearances than non-Aboriginal appearances result in a fine: namely 24.7 per cent compared with 36.1 per cent. Nevertheless, approximately similar proportions of both groups have benefited from the defaults payment program. Introduced as an option in 1980, this allows a child who fails to pay a fine within the stipulated time to undertake community work instead of detention. Of the 420 Aboriginal appearances which resulted in a fine during the period 1981–1984, 30.5 per cent were offered community work as a default option. The same applied to 28.1 per cent of the 3427 non-Aboriginal appearances which had a fine imposed. These minor differences are not significant. The value of a default option for a fine penalty is obvious. Most young Aborigines interviewed were either still at school or in receipt of unemployment benefits. Consequently, they found it extremely difficult to pay the average fine. Their ability to obtain financial assistance from family members was also limited because they generally came from single-parent households, whose sole source of income was the Supporting Parents Benefit.

(d) Discharge

The order of the Children's Court undoubtedly preferred by all young persons who appear before it is that of discharge without penalty. In this, the most lenient of all orders, Aborigines hold the advantage: in fact, 31.7

per cent of Aboriginal cases were discharged compared with 26.6 per cent of non-Aboriginal cases. Yet this should not be a cause for complacency. One suggestion made by social workers is that many young Aborigines should not be sent to Court in the first place and the Court is merely recognising this fact by discharging them. This suggestion is certainly consistent with the pattern of high referral rates of Aboriginal cases. In fact it lends considerable weight to the earlier evidence that Aboriginal youth is unjustly discriminated against by being sent to Court rather than to Aid Panels in such disproportionate numbers. This is especially important since an individual who is eventually discharged by the Court has nevertheless been subjected to the criminal justice process and, as a result of the Court appearance in which the allegations have been proved, will leave the system with a criminal record.

Why are the Penalties Different?

This pattern of Aboriginal over-representation at both the top and the bottom ends of the penalty scale (detention and discharge) is not explicable simply in terms of the nature of the offences with which they are charged. For example, taking break, enter, steal as the major charge, proportionately more Aboriginal than non-Aboriginal appearances resulted in detention: 7.8 per cent compared with 3.9 per cent respectively. At the same time, a higher proportion of Aboriginal than non-Aboriginal cases involving this allegation were discharged without penalty: 31.9 per cent and 24.8 per cent respectively.

Orders resulting from charges of common assault revealed a similar pattern; Aboriginal children received considerably more detention and suspended detention orders (11.4 per cent compared with 4.4 per cent respectively) than did their non-Aboriginal counterparts, as well as more discharges. Similar analyses were carried out for other major offence categories, and in each case comparable differences in penalties emerged. Thus, controlling for the major charge failed to explain differences between Aborigines and non-Aborigines in sentencing patterns. It is therefore not the offence which determines the different pattern of penalties awarded.

The explanation for differences in Court outcomes must thus be sought in factors other than the nature of the offence. Rigorous analysis of the sentencing process was not possible because of the statistical problems involved (see Appendix 20) and because of the complexity of the dispositional process itself. A wide range of information regarding the offending behaviour and the characteristics of the child are placed before the Court, much of which cannot be quantified. This applies particularly to the input by social workers in the various reports presented to the Court. Consequently, to ensure statistical validity, analysis of the sentencing procedure was confined to a limited group: Aboriginal youth resident in metropolitan Adelaide who were charged with break, enter, steal. Within this group, we sought to determine whether obvious factors, such as the individual's prior record or the presence of legal representation, co-varied with sentencing outcomes.

Interviews with Court personnel indicated that the most important factor influencing penalties is the child's record of previous Court appearances. This was supported by analysis of outcomes for young Aborigines resident in Adelaide who were charged with break, enter, steal. For this specific group, as the number of prior Court appearances increased, so did the likelihood of the most severe penalties: detention or suspended detention. In fact, no such orders were made in cases where a prior record did not exist. In contrast, 25.3 per cent of cases involving a prior Court record did result in detention or suspended detention. By contrast, the number of previous Aid Panel appearances had no significant effect on the likelihood of a detention outcome. Here again is clear evidence that decisions taken at an earlier stage of the criminal justice process permeate the whole system, including the dispositional stage. In particular, the Screening Panel decision to refer more Aborigines than non-Aborigines to Court increased the likelihood of a prior Court record which in turn could generate substantial disadvantage at the sentencing stage. Since the Screening Panel decision itself is heavily influenced by the initial decision to arrest, the compounding effect of police discretion is self-evident.

Of equal concern is the apparent role played by socio-economic factors in determining penalties. Again, unemployment and family structure proved to be related to Court outcomes. Cases involving unemployed Aboriginal youth were more likely to result in a detention order than were appearances by employed Aborigines (16.5 per cent compared with 9.2 per cent respectively). They were also less likely to be discharged without penalty (27.8 per cent compared with 41.8 per cent). The family structure within which the young Aboriginal lived at the time of apprehension also proved to be relevant to the Court outcome. No appearances by Aboriginal youth living in a nuclear two-parent household received a penalty of detention, while only 5.9 per cent resulted in suspended detention. In contrast, 9.7 per cent of appearances by Aboriginal youth living in 'other' family situations were sentenced to detention, while a further 8.2 per cent had their detention orders suspended.

This apparent link between unemployment, non-nuclear family situations and detention will inevitably result in greater disadvantage to Aboriginal youth than other youth, simply because, on a per capita basis, they are far more likely to be found in such socio-economic circumstances. This practice does not accord with the philosophy of the juvenile justice system. Under the terms of the legislation, it is proper for the Court to give particular consideration to the child's social and economic position, but not in a way which will disadvantage those already experiencing hardships. Instead, concern for the welfare of the child was designed to alleviate such disadvantage, not compound it by selecting these young people for harsher treatment. It quite clearly achieves the reverse of the legislative intention.

Different sentencing patterns also co-varied with the police decision to arrest rather than report a child. Again, taking appearances by Aborigines living in Adelaide charged with break, enter, steal, results indicated a significant correlation between penalties and the mode of apprehension. In particular, appearances based on arrest were more likely to result in detention or suspended detention. Thus, 10.6 per cent of Aboriginal appearances where an initial arrest had been made resulted in detention, compared with 3.8 per cent for reported cases. At the other end of the scale, appearances based on arrest had a lower chance of discharge than did other appearances: 30.4 per cent compared with 41.2 per cent respectively. Although this raises the possibility of a continuing carry-over effect of police decision-making at the point of apprehension, it is far more likely that the observed relationship is a spurious one, resulting from a strong association between arrest and prior Court records. In other words, an arrest increases the likelihood that the individual will be sent to Court, thereby acquiring a Court record. In turn, it is the existence of a Court record which, at any subsequent appearance, increases the likelihood of a detention order.

There is also a correlation between sentencing outcomes and the person presiding. Although the number of detentions imposed was similar, magistrates were more likely than judges to order detentions, but also were more likely to discharge a child without penalty. We found that 19.3 per cent of Aboriginal appearances before a magistrate resulted in some form of detention, compared with 15.2 per cent of Aboriginal appearances before a judge. At the other end of the scale, discharge without penalty accounted for 38.6 per cent of all appearances before a magistrate, but only 32.6 per cent of those coming before a judge. Since relatively more young Aborigines came before a magistrate than a judge, this might provide a partial explanation for their different sentencing patterns.

In contrast and rather surprisingly, legal representation did not seem to influence outcomes to any significant degree. Although a solicitor undoubtedly was of considerable value in a supportive role, in pre-trial negotiations and in ensuring that the child understood the Court process, he or she had no discernible effects on the orders awarded. This is important since the only aspect of the criminal justice process in which Aborigines are positively advantaged is access to legal representation.

Hidden Penalties

Apart from the actual sentence imposed by the Court, there may be additional penalties incurred by the individual which are not recorded in the official statistics. For example, Court costs are normally awarded against the accused when a fine is imposed and, at times, these costs exceed the amount of the fine. The judge or magistrate can also order compensation to be paid. In a recent Court hearing, a sixteen-year-old Aboriginal male was charged with assaulting police and resisting arrest. Although he claimed that the police had initiated the confrontation, he was found guilty but was discharged without penalty. Yet he was ordered to pay $21 compensation to one of the arresting officers for the purchase of a new tie ($6) and dry-cleaning costs ($15). The boy was also ordered to pay $86 compensation to the other officer for the purchase of a new pair of trousers to replace the pair torn while apprehending him. Thus, even though the young Aboriginal technically had no penalty imposed on him for the two 'street' offences, his subsequent failure to pay the $107 compensation costs could result in a warrant being issued for his arrest followed, in this case, by a five-day custodial period in a youth training centre. Unlike fines, neither Court costs nor compensation have a work default option. Failure to pay within the stipulated time means automatic detention, and since virtually no young Aborigines or their families are in a position to meet these additional financial burdens, such an outcome in many cases is inevitable.

Another form of compensation has recently been introduced in South Australia which is already having serious consequences for Aborigines. A levy of $10 per offence is now automatically payable by each offender to provide a general fund under the Criminal Injuries Compensation Scheme. This levy applies even when the offence is victimless, as in the case of offensive language or disorderly behaviour. It imposes yet another burden on Aboriginal youth and, as with other compensation orders, cannot be discharged by community work.

Thus, on the one hand, the juvenile justice system does its utmost to avoid imposing a direct sentence of detention on youth, and to this end, has carefully legislated for a fine default program so that young people unable to pay fines will not end up in detention. Yet on the other hand, the system imposes other costs which may result in a young offender spending time in a youth training centre. In such instances, children are penalised not for the original offence, but because they are too poor to pay.

Although not recorded in the official statistics, it is these hidden costs which are considered by Aborigines to be the most unjustifiable, especially since the amount of money involved can be considerable. This is illustrated by a breakdown of the total amount levied by the Children's Court against one fairly typical young Aboriginal over a period of time. Overall, this boy was ordered to pay $1057 to the Court. Yet only half of this, $575, involved actual fines imposed as a penalty. The remaining amount was made up of Court costs, victim levy, and compensation fees. Like many other young men in his position, he was unable to meet these costs and subsequently spent time in detention. These hidden costs inevitably contribute to the disproportionate number of young Aborigines being held in custody at any one time.

Conclusion

Young Aborigines are treated differently from other young people by the Children's Court process, but there is no clear evidence of racial bias operating as such. Indeed, they are given the apparent advantage of readier access to legal aid than other youth. Yet the disadvantage they suffer at the hands of the justice process is the product of the complex inter-relationship between the pre-Court and Court stages of that process as well as between various facets of the Court process itself. Large numbers of young Aborigines are denied access to Children's Aid Panels and are instead referred into the more formal Court system, where considerable delays may be experienced by accused individuals before the matter is determined by the Court. Some of these delays may involve deprivation of liberty. The delays may be well motivated — such as allowing time for the preparation of reports to assist the Court, and the preparation of the child's case by a lawyer — yet the costs to the individual must be weighed against the benefits.

At the ultimate stage of the Court process, namely sentencing, Aboriginal youth is over-represented at both the top and the bottom of the penalty scale. The high proportion of cases which are ultimately discharged may reflect an acknowledgement by the Court that such cases should not have been referred to it in the first place, but should more appropriately have been directed to an Aid Panel. The high number of Aboriginal discharges may indicate a deliberate attempt on the part of the Court to redress some of the accumulated disadvantage experienced by this group of young people.

However, notwithstanding this, a disproportionate number of detentions are ordered for Aborigines. Neither the nature of the charge nor the incidence of legal representation offers an adequate explanation for this. However, analysis did show that the initial police decision to arrest the offender at the point of entry into the criminal justice process seems to have an enduring, albeit indirect, effect at the final stage of disposition, through its influence on Screening Panel referral patterns. More young Aborigines were directed to Court because they were arrested, and in turn, this higher Court referral rate guaranteed more prior Court records and consequently stiffer penalties. Equally disturbing were the apparent effects on sentencing of unemployment and of non-nuclear family structure. There are indications that Aborigines receive harsher treatment at the sentencing stage of the juvenile justice process only coincidentally because they are Aborigines. Young Aboriginal women and men are more likely to be unemployed and less likely to live in nuclear-family households than other young people and are penalised for their already disadvantaged social position.

Looking at the whole operation of the juvenile justice process, it is clear that any disadvantage experienced by Aborigines at the sentencing stage can properly be seen as the end result of a compounding effect of numerous factors operating at earlier stages in the process. To show that the detention rate of Aboriginal youth is twenty-three times that of other youth virtually misses the real issue, as alarming as such a figure may sound. The crucial point is that throughout the whole process, right from the first contact with police, Aborigines are disadvantaged to an increasing degree, so that the final Court outcome is merely an inevitable result in a long chain of circumstances. Even though there is clear evidence that many participants in the system do all that is possible to try to achieve justice for Aborigines, the die is cast against equity right from the beginning. A crucial question must therefore be asked: why does a well-intentioned juvenile justice system seem incapable of ameliorating the position of a racial group who are already disadvantaged before they enter it?

8
Justice or Differential Treatment?

The juvenile justice system places its faith in the rehabilitation rather than the punishment of the individual child. In South Australia this trust rests in a process which seeks 'to secure for the child such care, protection, control, correction or guidance as will best lead to the proper development of his personality and to his development into a responsible and useful member of the community' (*Children's Protection and Young Offenders Act* 1979 section 7). But what does our society and its all-important institution, the criminal justice process, really offer to Aboriginal youth?

Young Aborigines are grossly over-represented in every sector of the juvenile justice system. Not only is their rate of apprehension disproportionately high compared with their relative numbers in the South Australian population, but moreover, at every stage within the system where discretion operates and individual decisions must be taken by the various agents of the law, they are substantially more likely than any other group to receive the harsher of the outcomes available. On a per capita basis, they are significantly more likely to be arrested by police rather than reported; to be referred by Screening Panels to the Children's Court, rather than being given the benefit of diversion to an Aid Panel; and finally, once before the Court, they experience more detention orders than any other ethnic group in the community. This remains true even when Aboriginal youth is compared with other highly visible minority groups such as Asians.

As a result of being over-represented at each level of the system, Aboriginal youths experience a process of accumulating differential, whereby the degree of disadvantage suffered by them becomes more pronounced as they move deeper into the system. Over-represented in relation to their population numbers by some seven times at the point of apprehension, their relative position deteriorates until, at the final point of detention, they are over-represented by some twenty-three times. No other ethnic group in South Australia experiences this phenomenon.

Yet within this framework of State-wide over-representation, the actual extent of their disadvantage varies dramatically from one region to another, from one town to another and even from one suburb to another within the same city. It is impossible to account for this in terms of behavioural differences amongst the young people, especially when there are marked differences in the judicial outcomes recorded for Aborigines living in adjacent rural communities, where lifestyles are similar. Nor is the extent of over-representation linked with the absolute size of the Aboriginal population or the proportion it forms in relation to the non-Aboriginal population. The only connection we could find was with the attitudes of the local community. Quite simply, Aborigines appear to be treated more severely by the justice system in areas where racial discrimination is highest. For example, on Yorke Peninsula, an area already noted for its adverse stereotypic views of Aborigines (Wundersitz, 1979a, 1979b), at the point of arrest Aboriginal youth is over-represented by some seventy-six times. This is in dramatic contrast with the Far Northern regions of South Australia where they are over-represented in arrest figures by only four times. Such wide variation seems to lead to the conclusion that justice operates differently in different locations, according to the degree of prejudice held by the white community.

It is, indeed, inevitable that agents of the system will be vulnerable to community pressures. In some areas where a good working relationship based on mutual respect has been established between police, welfare workers and the community, the over-representation of Aboriginal youth, especially at the point of arrest and Court referral, has been dramatically reduced. In some of these areas, workers have also adopted a policy of never recommending detention unless the Aboriginal community requests it, and as a result detention orders are seldom handed out. The judicial treatment of Aborigines in such locations stands out in stark contrast to that of other areas where prejudice is high, and where community pressure forces agents of the legal system to adopt a harsher approach towards local Aboriginal youth.

It is interesting that Aborigines in the more remote areas, where fewer white people live, fare a great deal better than those living in the more populated areas. Yet this is contrary to public expectation, which often seeks to explain Aboriginal over-involvement with legal mechanisms in terms of their remoteness.

It has been argued, for example, that for many rural Aborigines, it is necessary to arrest and bring them to the cities for processing because facilities cannot be provided in the remote areas. Yet this belief does not accord with the reality of the situation. The fact is that Aborigines living largely traditional lifestyles in those regions of the State where relatively few non-Aborigines live are actually treated more equitably in comparison with white youth than are Aborigines living within the general community. Ironically, it is in those areas where Aborigines live alongside whites that they seem to be most disadvantaged in terms of the extent and nature of their contact with 'the law'. This means that the more culturally assimilated they are into white society, the harsher may be their treatment by the justice system. The reason for this seems to lie in the fact that traditionally oriented Aborigines living on settlements and outstations in their own tribal country are recognised as culturally distinct. The community at large shows more sympathy towards these people who are considered to be 'real' Aborigines, and accepts that attempts should be made to accommodate their traditional values and lifestyles. Governments, through their various agencies, thus make special efforts to formulate policies and strategies which will better meet these needs. The establishment of a police aide scheme in the Pitjantjatjara lands is one example of this. Yet this same approach is not applied to those who have been forced to integrate into white society. There is no such willingness to recognise, let alone accommodate, the different cultural values of urban-based Aborigines.

The crucial question of whether Aborigines suffer disadvantage purely because they are Aboriginal admits no simple answer. In trying to come to grips with this issue, we focused on Aboriginal and non-Aboriginal youth who lived in comparable circumstances — in the State's capital city of Adelaide. At the point of apprehension, where police must decide whether to arrest or report a young individual, there was no clear evidence of racial bias once differences in charge profiles and socio-economic conditions were taken into account. Instead, the apparently differential treatment given to city-based Aboriginal youth compared with non-Aboriginal youth at this initial point of discretion could be explained by certain facts: firstly that young Aborigines were more likely to be unemployed and living in non-nuclear families than were non-Aborigines; and secondly, they were more likely to be charged with different, more serious offences and to have prior records of apprehension.

Yet rather than solving the original question as to whether police act in a discriminatory manner or not, this statistical result led to further questions. Why should the police decision to arrest be influenced by the social circumstances of a person, especially whether he or she is employed or living in a nuclear family? Such factors have no connection with the offending behaviour itself and inevitably disadvantage not only Aborigines but all other youths who do not conform with the middle-class ethos of mainstream society.

According to Police General Orders, the prime reason for arresting a child is to ensure that the accused attends Court. Unemployment and doubt about the accuracy of an address are used as key indicators of a person's reliability and therefore likelihood of voluntarily complying with a summons. Since most Aborigines are unemployed, they are instantly placed into that category of people whose reliability must be treated with suspicion. Yet criteria such as employment may not equate with what the

Aboriginal or any other minority group deems to be important. In Aboriginal society it is not occupational status which determines a person's social standing or reliability. Thus, young Aborigines are arrested in disproportionate numbers for social rather than criminal factors. Although not directly classifiable as racial discrimination, it nevertheless reflects the indirect effects of race through the operation of negative class stereotypes, and suggests that the whole operation of police discretion needs to be reassessed at this most fundamental level.

The second finding that the pattern of charging also determines the arrest decision seems, at least on the surface, to provide a more equitable basis for decision-making. However, there is no reasonable explanation as to why the charge profiles of Aborigines are so different, especially when comparisons are made only with non-Aborigines from similarly poor socio-economic backgrounds. As evidence of the enormous differences in charge profiles, of the 273 non-Aboriginal cases which matched the 273 Aboriginal cases on locational, demographic and economic characteristics, only 97 possessed comparable charge profiles. In other words, even within these small socio-economically matched groups, 176 out of 273 Aboriginal cases (i.e. 65 per cent) could not find a match from amongst the 273 non-Aboriginal cases in terms of the nature and number of offence charges laid or prior records of appearances.

Since these differences in charge patterns cannot be explained on socio-economic or residential grounds, it is difficult to escape the conclusion that racial prejudice is causing Aborigines to be charged differently. As other researchers, such as Cohen and Kluegel (1978: 173), have pointed out, although the charges laid and prior offending records are often accorded the status of 'fixed' legal variables, this is not so. Police have considerable discretion in determining who is to be charged and on what counts. Our concomitant qualitative studies in the form of household interviews, participant observations and discussions with young Aborigines, their mothers and lawyers led us to conclude that police charging practices may, in fact, be discriminatory. However, once the charges are laid down, the procedures which follow seem to be just, or at least predictable. If, for example, the records show that a young man has been charged with assaulting police, then on the surface this charge seems to justify an arrest. Yet this may conceal the fact that police initiated the confrontation with the boy which resulted in those charges being laid.

Inequitable forces were also identified at the next discretionary stage in the system, where Screening Panels operate as a pre-Court 'sifting' mechanism, determining the procedural future of a case. Here, definite statistical evidence of racial bias was forthcoming, with Panel members still choosing to select more Aboriginal than white youth for formal processing in the Children's Court, even when legal as well as socio-economic differences had been taken into account by comparing Aboriginal cases with a very small and highly selective 'matched' group of non-Aboriginal cases. Racial bias seemed to be most pronounced for those appearances brought about by way of a police report rather than an arrest. There was also clear evidence to suggest that members of Screening Panels base their decisions to refer Aborigines to Court on somewhat different criteria from those applied to non-Aborigines: a finding which also suggests the operation of racial bias.

Yet, perhaps more disturbing than any evidence of direct discrimination was the finding that in the majority of situations, the most important determinant of the Screening Panel referral was the method of apprehension. Quite categorically, young people who had been arrested by police were almost certain to be referred to Court, irrespective of the offending behaviour involved or their socio-economic and family circumstances.

It is thus patent that a decision taken at one level has significant repercussions at another. The inter-relationship between the various stages of the criminal justice process is thus a complex one, and the system creates its own momentum. The implications of that early police decision to arrest, rather than report, a child are far greater than police themselves realise at the time. The continuing impact of the arrest decision at the Screening Panel level provides an excellent example of the ineffectiveness of legislative reforms. In 1979 all arrested children were theoretically made eligible for diversion, and arrest is not even mentioned in the police or Community Welfare Department guidelines developed for Screening Panel determinations. Yet the stark fact is that most arrested children are sent to Court. Of course, this applies to all arrested children, irrespective of racial identity, but since far more Aboriginal children are arrested in the first place, the compounding effect of the system's own operation is self-evident. These findings tend to support the criticism commonly levelled against Screening Panels: that their constitution — and in particular, the presence of a police officer — may contribute to a lack of objectivity and independence in decision-making. If pre-trial filtering mechanisms such as Screening Panels are to continue, the legislative requirement that they be staffed by police obviously needs careful reappraisal, as does the overriding effect of police apprehension methods.

No aspect of the disadvantage suffered by young Aborigines in the course of the criminal justice process can give more cause for concern than their high rate of referral direct to Court. They are thereby denied access to a diversionary system for which South Australia has gained world-wide acclaim because of the opportunities it affords the individual to avoid re-offending and thus take a proper place in society: the principal aim of any juvenile justice system.

Clearly, Aid Panels cannot fulfil their intended role if relatively large numbers of young Aborigines are being denied access to the rehabilitative, non-stigmatising route which they offer. This is even more worrying because, unlike some other sectors of the justice system, those Aboriginal youths who do appear before Children's Aid Panels are treated no differently from their non-Aboriginal counterparts. Thus, it is not the Aid Panel system itself which is at fault, but the pre-Court 'sifting' mechanism. This is ironic because Screening Panels were specifically introduced to enable a social welfare perspective to be brought to bear, which was intended to further the rehabilitative goals of the legislation, not to compound the disadvantage of those youths already disadvantaged by their socio-economic status or ethnic identity. Once again, it is obvious that well-intentioned initiatives enshrined in legislation have failed in practice to deliver equity for Aboriginal youth.

By various routes, each adding disadvantage, Aborigines thus appear in Court substantially more often than do members of the mainstream society, even when comparisons are narrowed to a matched population with statistical controls regarding socio-economic and residential status.

At the disposition stage of the Children's Court hearing, differences were again evident. Young Aborigines are more likely than other young offenders to be sentenced to detention, and less likely to have that sentence suspended. In this they fail to benefit fully from current trends away from incarceration and in favour of more constructive alternatives. Although comprehensive statistical testing was not undertaken at this level, the most important determinant of a detention order seemed to be the child's prior record. In the main, the judges and magistrates presiding over the Children's Court did their utmost to avoid sentencing young people to detention, but once a young man or woman had come before them on a number of occasions, and the usual range of fines and bonds had been exhausted, a point was sometimes reached where detention seemed the only option. For a judge or magistrate, the constant reappearance of a young person before the Children's Court was taken as a clear sign that she or he was a recidivist who had failed to respond to the Court's attempts at rehabilitation, and that henceforth, detention was warranted to ensure the protection of the community and to provide correction. The fact that young Aborigines were generally more likely to have prior records thus largely explained their higher rate of detention.

Yet constant reappearance in Court does not necessarily indicate recidivism. Given the obvious disadvantage suffered by Aborigines at Screening Panel level, it is clear that many such children find themselves in Court for behaviour which, for another young person, would result in an Aid Panel appearance. The initial police decision to arrest a child, which virtually ensures a Court appearance and the subsequent acquisition of a criminal record, thus influences even the final sentencing stages of the Children's Court, and contributes to the disproportionately high number of detention orders imposed on young Aborigines.

Yet, although these detention rates are a matter of concern, this must not be allowed to obscure another important finding: the greater rate of referral to Court rather than to Aid Panels not only means a much greater chance of detention, but it also involves relatively more Aborigines in the whole formal Court process, which can, in itself, be quite punitive. Through the frequent use of adjournments, a particular matter may take months before finalisation. For Aboriginal youth in particular, these delays may involve custodial remands, which result in young people spending considerable periods in detention during the pre-sentencing stage of their Court process. Even if they are free on bail, frequent reappearances in Court impose considerable emotional and even economic pressure on the young person and her or his family. In many cases, they can become trapped in the system for months at a time by administrative or other forces over which they have little or no control. Such pre-sentence costs to the individual must be viewed very seriously. The relatively high proportion of young Aborigines who are eventually discharged by the Court is no matter for congratulation, for not only may the pre-trial costs to the individual have been great, but also society's concern may be that many such cases should not have been sent to Court in the first place.

The general assumption, certainly in the public mind, is that it is the Court process itself which is the cornerstone of the entire judicial system and that it is the judge or magistrate who makes the most crucial decision about a child's future, not the police or panelists. For adults, this may be true because of the essentially adversarial nature of the system, where emphasis is placed on establishing guilt and where the penalties which can be imposed may be quite severe, with the punishment fitting the crime. Yet it is patently not true of the juvenile justice system. In this jurisdiction, it is not the Court outcome or penalty which is necessarily critical to the girl or boy but the fact of having to appear in Court in the first place and thus becoming entangled in the highly formalised procedures. Usually, the penalty itself is not especially severe and in South Australia judges and magistrates clearly make every effort to help the young people who come before them. Detention is used only as a last resort. But justice at the point of sentencing has in many cases come too late.

Because the vast majority of young offenders plead guilty in the Children's Court, the very fact of being sent to Court virtually guarantees that the child will leave the system with a criminal record, which may have severe repercussions in adult life. It could therefore be argued that it is not the judge's decision regarding penalties which is critical, but the Screening Panel's decision to refer an offender to the Children's Court in the first place. In turn, that referral decision is predicated on the police decision to arrest rather than report a child. So in effect the most crucial decision made (once it has been decided that criminal proceedings should be launched) is that of the police at the very first level of the justice hierarchy. And this decision is often made by the most inexperienced and junior members of the police force who are most vulnerable to community pressure regarding race or class prejudices. So in juvenile justice the power hierarchy is inverted, with most power being vested in the lowest and least capable levels of the system. Yet decisions taken here influence the whole future of the person concerned and inadvertently countermand all later attempts to give equal opportunity to Aboriginal people.

This fact is not, it seems, widely recognised. The checks and balances which are built into the system to protect the rights of the individual accused and to ensure due process are primarily focused on the Court. At the Children's Court level, legal representation is permitted to ensure that the child's rights are protected: there is a system of reconsideration in place, whereby if a judge or magistrate imposes a particularly severe penalty on the child, the lawyer or social worker can, on his or her behalf, apply for the matter to be reconsidered by the Senior Judge of the Children's Court, which may result in a different penalty. This procedure ensures a high degree of accountability in the Court. No such safeguards are built into the earlier levels of decision-making. Screening Panel hearings are closed: no legal representation is permitted; there is no right of appeal. The child has no input into, or control over, the information which is placed before a Panel. The only type of check or balance is the facility to refer a matter to a judge for adjudication in the event that the police and Community Welfare representatives on the Panel cannot agree on an outcome. But such referrals can be initiated only by the panelists themselves and no outsider can apply for adjudication or review.

At the police level there is even less scrutiny. In theory, the arresting officer must obtain permission from his or her commissioned officer either before or immediately after the arrest has occurred. In practice, according to various police officers interviewed, this permission is viewed as a 'rubber stamp'. It is, apparently, easy to provide a superior officer with acceptable reasons for an arrest. Moreover, such accountability is an internal matter; police are required to justify their actions only to other police. There is no external means of monitoring and controlling the way police apply their discretion. Thus at the early stages, where the most crucial decisions are taken by the least experienced personnel, there are no mechanisms for external scrutiny.

Given the inter-connectedness of the various stages of the system and the finding that it is the early decision which overwhelmingly influences later decisions, it is obviously inadequate to focus only on the end stage, namely the penalties handed down by the Court. By this point, the damage has already been done. It also suggests that checks and balances at the Court level are no solution because they come too late. This may explain the apparent failure of the Aboriginal Legal Rights Movement to exert much positive effect on Children's Court outcomes. Access to legal representation is the one area where Aborigines are advantaged in comparison with other youth. It represents an example of positive discrimination, but one which is not all that effective, largely because it comes too late in the judicial process. It may, for example, be more beneficial for Aborigines to be legally represented at the Screening Panel stage to prevent them being sent to Court in the first place, rather than at the Court level. Again, it is a matter of too little, too late.

This book has been about differential treatment and not about different behaviour. Official crime statistics do not necessarily reflect actual behavioural patterns, but they do show how the official justice system itself operates in selecting and processing those individuals who are classed as suspects. Unlike many criminological studies, the book has not been concerned with identifying the causes of crime but with documenting how the system treats people once they are apprehended.

It has taken South Australia as a case study because that is the only State where detailed long-term statistics are available. The extremely disadvantaged position described for Aboriginal youth in South Australia does not mean that the situation in this State is in any way atypical: in fact, from what comparable information is available, it appears that the position in many other States may be worse. The maintaining of detailed statistics on youth offending in South Australia may, of itself, show that State's desire to ensure equity in the system's operation. Administrations which do not maintain such data may be largely unaware of the problems which exist or be unable to decipher them. This study merely shows that, in the only place where detailed records are available over a lengthy period, the situation for young Aborigines is very bad in spite of numerous efforts to improve it.

Several conclusions stand out from this analysis of juvenile justice. The most important is the clear evidence that legislative reform does not always deliver the social justice to which it aspires. In some instances, changes actually produce an opposite effect and worsen the situation for those they are intended to help. For example, the introduction of Children's Aid Panels has seemingly brought more children into official contact with the criminal justice process, albeit at pre-trial level. And whilst legislative change has declared, at least in theory, that arrested children are now eligible for diversion, in fact few are given this opportunity. Practice has not followed the theory.

Yet despite these findings, changes to the legislation are still being undertaken. In 1988, the South Australian legislation was amended by adding to the list of relevant factors 'the child's ethnic or racial background and the need to guard against damage to the child's sense of cultural identity': *Children's Protection and Young Offenders Act Amendment Act* 1988 (S.A.). This innovation has been made primarily for matters involving children in need of care, although in practice it may well be invoked in criminal proceedings also. As yet, it is too early to analyse its practical effect or to determine whether, like some other legislative changes, it will have the opposite result from that intended.

Clearly, great care must therefore be taken to ensure that the operation of the legal system does not serve to worsen the plight of those already disadvantaged in society.

Those involved in the operation of the criminal justice system should also be aware of the complex relationships between the different stages of the process and of the impact of decisions taken at one stage on an individual's progress through subsequent stages of the system. We must not only recognise the existence of disadvantage; we must also make sure that we do not unintentionally compound it.

The large element of discretion inherent in and essential to the operation of a juvenile justice system carries with it dangers as well as benefits, in that the prejudices of the decision-maker may determine the decision. This can operate in many ways and class prejudice can be just as influential as racial prejudice in the decision-making. Where the two coincide, as in the case of so many young Aborigines, the result can be disastrous.

Our crucial findings — that the initial arrest decision, the facts of being unemployed and living in a household other than a nuclear family crucially influence those decisions taken by agents of the juvenile justice process — are not race-specific. But they are features far more common to young Aborigines than to other children. Thus, although steps have been taken in recent years to improve the South Australian juvenile justice system, Aborigines are already disadvantaged when they enter it, and the very ways in which they are disadvantaged are used by the system itself to compound that disadvantage.

The current philosophy of the juvenile justice system, which reflects a mixed model based on both welfare and justice, undoubtedly operates well for a large proportion of South Australian youth. But that proportion is basically drawn from the middle classes. The system requires middle-class characteristics such as parental care in nuclear households and employment status in order for it to operate to the benefit of the child. The Western middle-class concept on which the system is based requires various characteristics that simply do not apply to many Aboriginal families. Yet this does not mean that Aboriginal families are more criminal; merely, that they are poor and often have different values and lifestyles.

Factors such as residential mobility and large multi-unit households so typical of the Aboriginal community, represent positive adaptive mechanisms which allow Aborigines to cope more successfully with urban life and to manipulate their environment to maximise their otherwise limited economic and social resources (Gale and Wundersitz, 1982). Yet it is these very characteristics which are used by administrators of the justice system to justify the differentially harsher treatment of apprehended Aboriginal youth.

These findings of substantial disadvantage for Aboriginal youth are not at all at variance with the legislation. Thus a justice system which is predicated on Western middle-class values, even one as progressive as South Australia's is said to be, seems to be unable to offer equitable treatment for socially disadvantaged coloured minorities.

Appendixes

Appendix 1

The South Australian Young Offenders' File: a description of variables

Three groups of variables were collected. The first involved details relating to each separate charge (up to a maximum of eight charges per appearance). These included the type and nature of the charge, the plea recorded for that charge, the penalty imposed (including discharge without penalty) and, if applicable, the duration of that penalty. The major charge was distinguished from the charge attracting the major penalty, as were the associated pleas, penalties and penalty duration.

Secondly, details regarding the actual 'mechanics' of the appearance were noted, such as the date and geographic location of the hearing, the method of apprehension, whether it took place before an Aid Panel or Court, whether legal representation was present, whether the person presiding was a judge or magistrate, and the number of adjournments.

The third set of variables related to the individual. These included information on previous contact with the welfare or justice systems, such as the number of previous Aid Panel or Court appearances, and whether the young person was under the care of the State, was subject to an existing order, or was an absconder. Social background details relating to age, gender, residential address, education level, family structure, current and previous occupations and identity (i.e. whether Aboriginal or non-Aboriginal) were also recorded, as were the occupation, income, marital status and ethnic identity of the parent(s).

Appendix 2

Major offence charge: internal distribution of cases and the percentage brought about by way of an arrest

Major offence charge	Distribution % (n = 7156)	% of cases based on arrest
Drunk in public place	1.0	73.6
Disorderly, offensive behaviour	4.1	50.5
Break, enter with intent	1.3	41.5
Motor vehicle theft	6.2	40.0
Break, enter, steal	10.9	38.6
Common assault	4.3	23.5
No licence	1.5	16.7
Wilful damage	3.5	15.4
Use or possess drugs	4.6	13.3
Receiving	2.1	12.8
Larceny	13.0	12.6
Unlawfully on premises	1.4	8.8
False pretences	1.2	6.0
Minor consuming, obtaining liquor	2.4	4.0
Carry offensive weapon	1.6	3.5
Shoplifting	28.2	0.1

Appendix 3

Legal variables: internal distribution of cases and the percentage based on arrest

Legal variables	Distribution %	% of cases based on arrest
No. of offence charges		
1	71.8	10.4
2	16.2	31.0
3 or more	12.1	46.6
	(n = 7156)	
No. of prior Aid Panel appearances		
0	74.7	9.1
1–2	16.5	36.1
3 or more	8.8	60.0
	(n = 7156)	
No. of prior Court appearances		
0	60.1	6.9
1–2	29.7	27.5
3 or more	10.2	56.0
	(n = 7156)	
Subject to existing order		
Yes	6.5	58.9
No	93.5	15.2
	(n = 7156)	

Appendix 4

Personal and socio-economic factors: internal distribution of cases and the percentage based on arrest

Personal and socio-economic factors	Distribution %	% of cases based on arrest
Age in years		
10	1.6	4.5
11–12	10.5	4.8
13–14	30.6	9.5
15–16	37.4	23.1
17	19.9	29.6
	(n = 7121)	
Sex		
Male	75.8	21.4
Female	24.2	7.6
	(n = 7156)	
Family structure		
Nuclear family	63.7	9.3
Single-parent family	26.7	17.7
Relatives, foster parents	4.1	26.1
Other	5.5	37.7
	(n = 6313)	
Occupational status		
Unemployed	23.0	33.0
Employed	11.8	18.1
Student	65.2	7.3
	(n = 6432)	
Residential location		
Port Adelaide (low status)	6.4	23.1
Marion (lower-middle status)	6.8	17.5
Burnside (upper status)	1.4	11.8
	(n = 7156)	

Appendix 5

Reassessment of the relationship between identity and the method of apprehension using one control factor

Control variable	Zero-order gamma	First-order partial gamma
No. of offence charges	.63766	.63242
No. of previous Aid Panel appearances	.63766	.44585
No. of previous Court appearances	.63766	.47439
Absconder or under an existing order	.63766	.62599
Family structure	.65971	.57656
Occupational status	.65916	.65291

In this table, the zero-order gamma measures the original strength of association when no controls are used, while the first-order partial gamma reassesses that relationship while partialling out the effects of the specified control variable. A large reduction in the partial gamma would indicate that the original relationship between racial identity and the method of apprehension is a spurious one brought about by the mutual association of these two variables with the specified control variable.

Two variables, namely the major charge and residential address, are not included in this table. Since both of these characteristics represent nominal-level measurements only, and since there was no way of dichotomising them to produce a ratio measurement (as was done with family structure and occupational status), summary gamma values could not appropriately be generated for them.

Of the controls which were used, three — namely, the number of offence charges, whether the child was an absconder or under an existing Court order, and occupational status — produced only a very slight weakening in the strength of relationship between racial identity and the method of apprehension. Larger reductions were observed when the effects of family structure, the number of prior Court appearances and the number of prior Aid Panel appearances were separately partialled out, thus indicating that each provided at least some explanation for the disproportionately high arrest rates recorded for Aboriginal youth. Nevertheless, in each case, the first-order partial gamma remained sufficiently large to indicate a significant relationship between identity and apprehension modes, irrespective of which control factor was used.

Appendix 6

The matching process: a comment

The procedure used here actually reduced the scale and to some extent changed the nature of the analysis. From the overall total of 6000 non-Aboriginal appearances, the matching process selected only that number (273) required to match exactly each of the Aboriginal appearances according to age, gender, family structure, occupation and address. Consequently, the Aboriginal group is now being compared, not with the non-Aboriginal group as a whole, but instead with this small selected sub-group. Moreover, this small sub-group of non-Aborigines, because of the very nature of the matching process, will exhibit a significantly different social and demographic profile from that of the total non-Aboriginal group. Thus, just as the 273 Aboriginal appearances involved a significantly higher proportion of youth who were unemployed, who came from a non-nuclear family and who lived in the poorer suburbs of Adelaide than did non-Aboriginal appearances as a whole, so will the matched sample of non-Aborigines differ in the same way and to the same extent from all non-Aboriginal appearances.

In effect then, matching with Aboriginal appearances on background factors has produced a sub-group of white youth from the lower end of the socio-economic scale along which non-Aboriginal young offenders as a whole are ranged.

Appendix 7

Logistic regression analysis: a brief description

In logistic regression analysis, the dichotomised variable of arrest or non-arrest constituted the dependent variable (i.e. the outcome we are trying to predict) while the four legal variables of the major charge, the number of offence charges and the number of previous Court and Aid Panel appearances formed the independent or predictor variables. In logistic regression analysis, an independent variable is retained in the statistical model only if it exerts a significant effect on the dependent variable (in this case, the decision to arrest) which is additional to that contributed by the other variables tested. Conversely, those which do not make an independent contribution are eliminated from the analysis. Any spurious correlations are thereby identified. The logistic regression procedure also generates a probability table which predicts the probability of arrest for every possible combination of variables retained in the analysis. These probabilities are calculated from the fitted logistic model. The underlying assumption of this model is that the regression line holds across the data. Thus, if the data are grouped at one end of the continuum, it is assumed that the trend present in that data and represented by the fitted regression line will continue on, even when the line is projected beyond the data.

Appendix 8

Probability of arrest for Aboriginal appearances

Major charge		No previous appearances before Aid Panel			1–2 previous appearances before Aid Panel			3 or more previous appearances before Aid Panel		
		C0	C1–2	C3+	C0	C1–2	C3+	C0	C1–2	C3+
Larceny	Of1	0.041	0.078	0.111	0.115	0.204	0.275	0.133	0.233	0.310
	Of2	0.076	0.140	0.193	0.199	0.330	0.421	0.228	0.369	0.464
	Of3+	0.096	0.173	0.236	0.243	0.388	0.484	0.276	0.430	0.527
Break, enter	Of1	0.096	0.174	0.237	0.244	0.389	0.485	0.277	0.431	0.528
	Of2	0.169	0.287	0.374	0.382	0.550	0.644	0.424	0.593	0.683
	Of3+	0.208	0.342	0.435	0.444	0.612	0.700	0.487	0.652	0.735
Vehicle theft	Of1	0.137*	0.240*	0.318*	0.326*	0.489*	0.586*	0.365*	0.532*	0.627*
	Of2	0.234	0.377	0.472	0.481*	0.647*	0.731*	0.524*	0.686	0.763
	Of3+	0.283*	0.438	0.535	0.545*	0.703*	0.778*	0.587*	0.738	0.806
Assault	Of1	0.072*	0.133	0.184	0.190*	0.317*	0.407*	0.218*	0.355	0.449
	Of2	0.129	0.227	0.302	0.310	0.471	0.568	0.348	0.514	0.610
	Of3+	0.161	0.274	0.359	0.367	0.534	0.629	0.408	0.577	0.668
Disorderly behaviour	Of1	0.193	0.321	0.411	0.420	0.589	0.679	0.463	0.630	0.716
	Of2	0.314	0.475	0.573	0.582	0.733	0.802	0.623	0.766	0.828
	Of3+	0.371	0.539	0.633	0.642	0.780	0.840	0.680	0.808	0.862
Shoplifting	Of1	0.000	0.000	0.000	0.000	0.000	0.000	0.000	0.000	0.000
	Of2	0.000	0.000	0.000	0.000	0.000	0.000	0.000	0.000	0.000
	Of3+	0.000	0.000	0.000	0.000	0.000	0.000	0.000	0.000	0.001
Other	Of1	0.156*	0.268*	0.351*	0.360*	0.526*	0.621*	0.400*	0.569*	0.661*
	Of2	0.262*	0.413	0.509*	0.519*	0.681*	0.759*	0.562*	0.717*	0.789*
	Of3+	0.314*	0.475*	0.572*	0.581*	0.733*	0.802*	0.623*	0.765*	0.828*

Note: in Appendixes 8, 9, 15, 16, 18 and 19, the number of Aid Panel appearances is set across the top, and within each Panel appearance grouping, the number of prior Court appearances is detailed. C0 therefore refers to no previous appearances before the Children's Court; C1–2 refers to 1 or 2 prior Court appearances and C3+ refers to three or more prior Court appearances. The major charge is listed down the left hand side of the table and for each charge category, the number of offences listed for the current appearance (i.e. 1, 2, 3 and over) is detailed.
*Indicates situations in which the predicted probability of an arrest for Aboriginal youth exceeded that of non-Aboriginal youth by at least 10 chances in 100.

Appendix 9

Probability of arrest for matched non-Aboriginal appearances

Major charge		No previous appearances before Aid Panel			1–2 previous appearances before Aid Panel			3 or more previous appearances before Aid Panel		
		C0	C1–2	C3+	C0	C1–2	C3+	C0	C1–2	C3+
Larceny	Of1	0.043	0.134	0.180	0.076	0.221	0.288	0.117	0.314	0.395
	Of2	0.160	0.398	0.484	0.259	0.548	0.633	0.361	0.662	0.736
	Of3+	0.185	0.441	0.528	0.294	0.591	0.673	0.402	0.700	0.769
Break, enter	Of1	0.096	0.269	0.344	0.163	0.403	0.490	0.239	0.522	0.608
	Of2	0.312	0.611	0.691	0.454	0.743	0.804	0.573	0.824	0.869
	Of3+	0.350	0.652	0.727	0.498	0.775	0.830	0.616	0.848	0.888
Vehicle theft	Of1	0.039	0.122	0.165	0.069	0.204	0.267	0.106	0.292	0.370
	Of2	0.146	0.373	0.459	0.239	0.522	0.609	0.337	0.638	0.715
	Of3+	0.170	0.415	0.502	0.273	0.566	0.650	0.377	0.678	0.750
Assault	Of1	0.063	0.191	0.251	0.111	0.302	0.381	0.167	0.411	0.499
	Of2	0.225	0.502	0.589	0.347	0.649	0.724	0.462	0.749	0.809
	Of3+	0.257	0.545	0.631	0.388	0.688	0.758	0.506	0.781	0.835
Disorderly behaviour	Of1	0.617	0.848	0.888	0.747	0.911	0.936	0.827	0.943	0.959
	Of2	0.873	0.960	0.971	0.927	0.978	0.984	0.953	0.986	0.990
	Of3+	0.891	0.966	0.976	0.938	0.981	0.987	0.960	0.988	0.992
Shoplifting	Of1	0.000	0.000	0.000	0.000	0.000	0.000	0.000	0.000	0.000
	Of2	0.000	0.000	0.001	0.000	0.001	0.001	0.000	0.001	0.002
	Of3+	0.000	0.000	0.001	0.000	0.001	0.001	0.000	0.001	0.002
Other	Of1	0.031	0.099	0.135	0.055	0.168	0.223	0.086	0.246	0.317
	Of2	0.119	0.319	0.400	0.199	0.463	0.551	0.286	0.582	0.664
	Of3+	0.139	0.359	0.443	0.228	0.507	0.594	0.323	0.624	0.702

Appendix 10

Results of log-linear analysis for Aboriginal and non-Aboriginal youth

Step no.	Term	Degrees of freedom	Log likelihood	Goodness of fit Chi square	p value	Improvement Chi square	p value
Aboriginal							
0	Constant	—	−141.426	263.445	0.225	—	—
1	Occupation	2	−132.493	245.578	0.514	17.866	0.000
2	Sex	1	−129.622	239.836	0.599	5.742	0.017
Non-Aboriginal							
0	Constant	—	−1502.950	2108.693	0.812	—	—
1	Occupation	2	−1465.682	2034.169	0.978	74.535	0.000
2	Family	2	−1455.929	2014.662	0.989	19.506	0.000
3	Age	2	−1450.430	2003.662	0.993	10.998	0.004

Appendix 11

Major offence charge: internal distribution of cases and percentage referred to the Children's Court

Major charge	Distribution % (n = 7156)	% of cases referred to court
Disorderly, offensive behaviour	4.1	64.7
Motor vehicle theft	6.2	64.3
Common assault	4.3	62.5
Break, enter, steal	10.9	59.1
Larceny	13.0	50.3
Use or possess drugs	4.6	48.3
Wilful damage	3.5	40.2
Receiving	2.1	38.5
Unlawfully on premises	1.4	36.3
Minor consuming, obtaining liquor	2.4	33.5
Carry offensive weapon	1.6	19.1
Shoplifting	28.2	0

Appendix 12

Legal variables: internal distribution of cases and the percentage referred to the Children's Court

Legal variables	Distribution %	% of cases referred to court
No. of offence charges		
1	71.7	25.0
2	16.2	59.8
3 or more	12.1	79.3
	(n = 7156)	
No. of prior Aid Panel appearances		
0	74.7	19.7
1–2	16.5	84.0
3 or more	8.8	98.1
	(n = 7156)	
No. of prior Court appearances		
0	60.1	10.3
1–2	29.7	70.9
3 or more	10.2	97.5
	(n = 7156)	
Subject to existing order		
Yes	6.5	100.0
No	93.5	32.9
	(n = 7156)	
Method of apprehension		
Arrest	18.1	94.7
Report	81.9	24.5
	(n = 7156)	

Appendix 13

Personal and socio-economic factors: internal distribution of cases and the percentage referred to the Children's Court

Personal and socio-economic factors	Distribution %	% of cases referred to court
Age in years		
10	1.6	12.5
11–12	10.5	14.2
13–14	30.6	22.8
15–16	37.4	45.4
17	19.9	57.5
	(n = 7121)	
Sex		
Male	75.8	44.3
Female	24.2	15.0
	(n = 7156)	
Family structure		
Nuclear family	63.7	22.4
Single-parent family	26.7	37.7
Foster parents or with relatives	4.1	47.5
Other	5.5	66.1
	(n = 6313)	
Occupational status		
Student	65.2	18.3
Employed	11.8	40.3
Unemployed	23.0	62.0
	(n = 6432)	
Residential location		
Port Adelaide (low status)	6.4	46.4
Enfield (low status)	11.0	43.9
Elizabeth (low status)	6.3	43.8
Marion (lower-middle status)	6.8	35.9
Unley (middle status)	2.4	35.7
Burnside (upper status)	1.4	25.5
	(n = 7156)	

Appendix 14

Reassessment of the relationship between identity and referral outcome using one control factor

Control variable	Zero-order gamma	First-order partial gamma
Number of offence charges	.67973	.64166
Number of previous Aid Panel appearances	.67973	.48549
Number of previous Court appearances	.67973	.56030
Under an existing order	.67973	.61669
Mode of apprehension	.61832	.56926
Family structure	.66853	.59389
Occupational status	.68613	.67473

This table summarises the results obtained from re-analysing the relationship between Court referral and racial identity while controlling separately for each of seven co-variant factors. As shown, in each case there was some reduction in the strength of the association between identity and referral, indicating that each factor provided at least a partial explanation for the high Court referral rates recorded by Aboriginal youth. Yet in each situation, the first-order partial gamma remained sufficiently large to indicate the retention of a significant relationship between identity and referral patterns, irrespective of which control variable is used. Although neither the major offence charge nor residential address are included in this table for reasons already given (Chapter 5), nevertheless, irrespective of which charge or which suburban location is considered, Aboriginal cases were still significantly more likely to be directed to Court than non-Aboriginal cases. Thus, neither the nature of the offence nor the address of the individual can explain the high Court referral rates recorded for young Aborigines.

Appendix 15

Probability of a Court referral for Aboriginal appearances based on arrest

Major charge		No previous appearances before Aid Panel			1–2 previous appearances before Aid Panel			3 or more previous appearances before Aid Panel		
		C0	C1–2	C3+	C0	C1–2	C3+	C0	C1–2	C3+
Larceny	Of1	0.885*	0.988	0.998	0.983*	0.998	1.000	0.962*	0.996	0.999
	Of2	0.885	0.988	0.998	0.983	0.998	1.000	0.962	0.996	0.999
	Of3+	0.885	0.988	0.998	0.983	0.998	1.000	0.962	0.996	0.999
Break, enter	Of1	0.837*	0.982	0.997	0.975*	0.998	1.000	0.944*	0.994	0.999
	Of2	0.837	0.982	0.997	0.975*	0.998	1.000	0.944	0.994	0.999
	Of3+	0.837	0.982	0.997	0.975	0.998	1.000	0.944	0.994	0.999
Vehicle theft	Of1	0.811	0.978	0.996	0.970*	0.997	0.999	0.934*	0.993	0.999
	Of2	0.811	0.978	0.996	0.970	0.997	0.999	0.934	0.993	0.999
	Of3+	0.811	0.978	0.996	0.970	0.997	0.999	0.934	0.993	0.999
Assault	Of1	0.906	0.990	0.998	0.986*	0.999	1.000	0.969*	0.997	0.999
	Of2	0.906	0.990	0.998	0.986	0.999	1.000	0.969	0.997	0.999
	Of3+	0.906	0.990	0.998	0.986	0.999	1.000	0.969	0.997	0.999
Disorderly behaviour	Of1	0.677*	0.957	0.992	0.941*	0.994*	0.999	0.874*	0.986	0.998
	Of2	0.677*	0.957	0.992	0.941*	0.994	0.999	0.874*	0.986	0.998
	Of3+	0.677	0.957	0.992	0.941*	0.994	0.999	0.874*	0.986	0.998
Shoplifting	Of1	0.000	0.003	0.019	0.002	0.025	0.126	0.001	0.011	0.059
	Of2	0.000	0.003	0.019	0.002	0.025	0.126	0.001	0.011	0.059
	Of3+	0.000	0.003	0.019	0.002	0.025	0.126	0.001	0.011	0.059
Other	Of1	0.726*	0.966	0.994	0.953*	0.995	0.999	0.898*	0.989	0.998
	Of2	0.726	0.966	0.994	0.953*	0.995	0.999	0.898*	0.989	0.998
	Of3+	0.726	0.966	0.994	0.953*	0.995	0.999	0.898*	0.989	0.998

*Indicates situations in which the predicted probability of a Court referral for Aboriginal youth exceeded that of non-Aboriginal youth by at least 10 chances in 100.

Appendix 16

Probability of a Court referral for non-Aboriginal appearances based on arrest

Major charge		No previous appearances before Aid Panel			1–2 previous appearances before Aid Panel			3 or more previous appearances before Aid Panel		
		C0	C1–2	C3+	C0	C1–2	C3+	C0	C1–2	C3+
Larceny	Of1	0.785	0.991	0.998	0.785	0.991	0.998	0.785	0.991	0.998
	Of2	0.944	0.998	1.000	0.944	0.998	1.000	0.944	0.998	1.000
	Of3+	0.956	0.998	1.000	0.956	0.998	1.000	0.956	0.998	1.000
Break, enter	Of1	0.587	0.977	0.994	0.587	0.977	0.994	0.587	0.977	0.994
	Of2	0.867	0.995	0.999	0.867	0.995	0.999	0.867	0.995	0.999
	Of3+	0.894	0.996	0.999	0.894	0.996	0.999	0.894	0.996	0.999
Vehicle theft	Of1	0.762	0.990	0.997	0.762	0.990	0.997	0.762	0.990	0.997
	Of2	0.936	0.998	0.999	0.936	0.998	0.999	0.936	0.998	0.999
	Of3+	0.950	0.998	1.000	0.950	0.998	1.000	0.950	0.998	1.000
Assault	Of1	0.842	0.994	0.998	0.842	0.994	0.998	0.842	0.994	0.998
	Of2	0.961	0.999	1.000	0.961	0.999	1.000	0.961	0.999	1.000
	Of3+	0.969	0.999	1.000	0.969	0.999	1.000	0.969	0.999	1.000
Disorderly behaviour	Of1	0.228	0.898	0.972	0.228	0.898	0.972	0.228	0.898	0.972
	Of2	0.575	0.976	0.994	0.575	0.976	0.994	0.575	0.976	0.994
	Of3+	0.635	0.981	0.995	0.635	0.981	0.995	0.635	0.981	0.995
Shoplifting	Of1	0.000	0.013	0.048	0.000	0.013	0.048	0.000	0.013	0.048
	Of2	0.002	0.055	0.188	0.002	0.055	0.188	0.002	0.055	0.188
	Of3+	0.003	0.070	0.230	0.003	0.070	0.230	0.003	0.070	0.230
Other	Of1	0.377	0.948	0.986	0.377	0.948	0.986	0.377	0.948	0.986
	Of2	0.736	0.988	0.997	0.736	0.988	0.997	0.736	0.988	0.997
	Of3+	0.782	0.991	0.998	0.782	0.991	0.998	0.782	0.991	0.998

Appendix 17

Arrest-based appearances: Probability of Court referral for those charged with one offence only, and no record of a previous Court appearance (chances per 100)

Major charge	No previous appearances before Aid Panel		1–2 previous appearances before Aid Panel		3 or more previous appearances before Aid Panel	
	Abs.	non-Abs.	Abs.	non-Abs.	Abs.	non-Abs.
Larceny	89	79	98	79	96	79
Break, enter, steal	84	59	98	59	94	59
Vehicle theft	81	76	97	76	93	76
Assault	91	84	99	84	97	84
Disorderly behaviour	68	23	94	23	87	23

The figures presented in this table have been extracted from Appendixes 15 and 16.

Appendix 18

Probability of a Court referral for Aboriginal appearances based on reports

Major charge		No previous appearance before Aid Panel			1–2 previous appearances before Aid Panel			3 or more previous appearances before Aid Panel		
		C0	C1–2	C3+	C0	C1–2	C3+	C0	C1–2	C3+
Larceny	Of1	0.145	0.641	0.909	0.562*	0.931*	0.987	0.358*	0.855*	0.971
	Of2	0.145	0.641	0.909	0.562*	0.931	0.987	0.358	0.855	0.971
	Of3+	0.145	0.641	0.909	0.562*	0.931	0.987	0.358	0.855	0.971
Break, enter	Of1	0.102	0.545	0.871	0.462*	0.901*	0.981*	0.272*	0.798*	0.957*
	Of2	0.102	0.545	0.871	0.462*	0.901	0.981	0.272*	0.798	0.957
	Of3+	0.102	0.545	0.871	0.462*	0.901	0.981	0.272*	0.798	0.957
Vehicle theft	Of1	0.086	0.500	0.849	0.418*	0.884*	0.977	0.238*	0.768	0.949
	Of2	0.086	0.500	0.849	0.418*	0.884	0.977	0.238	0.768	0.949
	Of3+	0.086	0.500	0.849	0.418*	0.884	0.977	0.238	0.768	0.949
Assault	Of1	0.174	0.690	0.926	0.616*	0.944*	0.990	0.411*	0.880*	0.976
	Of2	0.174	0.690	0.926	0.616*	0.944	0.990	0.411	0.880	0.976
	Of3+	0.174	0.690	0.926	0.616*	0.944	0.990	0.411	0.880	0.976
Disorderly behaviour	Of1	0.044	0.327*	0.732*	0.259*	0.787*	0.954*	0.132*	0.616*	0.900*
	Of2	0.044	0.327	0.732	0.259*	0.787*	0.954*	0.132*	0.616*	0.900*
	Of3+	0.044	0.327	0.732	0.259*	0.787*	0.954*	0.132*	0.616	0.900
Shoplifting	Of1	0.000	0.000	0.000	0.000	0.001	0.003	0.000	0.000	0.001
	Of2	0.000	0.000	0.000	0.000	0.001	0.003	0.000	0.000	0.001
	Of3+	0.000	0.000	0.000	0.000	0.001	0.003	0.000	0.000	0.001
Other	Of1	0.055	0.382*	0.776*	0.307*	0.824*	0.964*	0.162*	0.671*	0.920*
	Of2	0.055	0.382	0.776	0.307*	0.824*	0.964	0.162*	0.671	0.920
	Of3+	0.055	0.382	0.776	0.307*	0.824*	0.964	0.162	0.671	0.920

*Indicates situations in which the predicted probability of a Court referral for Aboriginal youth exceeded that of non-Aboriginal youth by at least 10 chances in 100.

Appendix 19

Probability of a Court referral for non-Aboriginal appearances based on reports

Major charge		No previous appearances before Aid Panel			1–2 previous appearances before Aid Panel			3 or more previous appearances before Aid Panel		
		C0	C1–2	C3+	C0	C1–2	C3+	C0	C1–2	C3+
Larceny	Of1	0.075	0.707	0.906	0.075	0.707	0.906	0.075	0.707	0.906
	Of2	0.271	0.917	0.978	0.271	0.917	0.978	0.271	0.917	0.978
	Of3+	0.323	0.935	0.983	0.323	0.935	0.983	0.323	0.935	0.983
Break, enter	Of1	0.030	0.484	0.789	0.030	0.484	0.789	0.030	0.484	0.789
	Of2	0.126	0.812	0.945	0.126	0.812	0.945	0.126	0.812	0.945
	Of3+	0.156	0.847	0.957	0.156	0.847	0.957	0.156	0.847	0.957
Vehicle theft	Of1	0.066	0.678	0.893	0.066	0.678	0.893	0.066	0.678	0.893
	Of2	0.245	0.906	0.975	0.245	0.906	0.975	0.245	0.906	0.975
	Of3+	0.294	0.926	0.980	0.294	0.926	0.980	0.294	0.926	0.980
Assault	Of1	0.105	0.779	0.933	0.105	0.779	0.933	0.105	0.779	0.933
	Of2	0.351	0.942	0.985	0.351	0.942	0.985	0.351	0.942	0.985
	Of3+	0.410	0.954	0.988	0.410	0.954	0.988	0.410	0.954	0.988
Disorderly behaviour	Of1	0.006	0.163	0.436	0.006	0.163	0.436	0.006	0.163	0.436
	Of2	0.029	0.472	0.780	0.029	0.472	0.780	0.029	0.472	0.780
	Of3+	0.037	0.534	0.820	0.037	0.534	0.820	0.037	0.534	0.820
Shoplifting	Of1	0.000	0.000	0.001	0.000	0.000	0.001	0.000	0.000	0.001
	Of2	0.000	0.001	0.005	0.000	0.001	0.005	0.000	0.001	0.005
	Of3+	0.000	0.002	0.007	0.000	0.002	0.007	0.000	0.002	0.007
Other	Of1	0.013	0.286	0.614	0.013	0.286	0.614	0.013	0.286	0.614
	Of2	0.058	0.648	0.880	0.058	0.648	0.880	0.058	0.648	0.880
	Of3+	0.073	0.702	0.904	0.073	0.702	0.904	0.073	0.702	0.904

Appendix 20

Analysing Children's Court outcomes: some statistical problems

In Chapters 5 and 6, a precise evaluation was made of the contribution of a number of variables to the differential rates of Aboriginal arrest and Court referrals by using matched sampling and logistic regression analysis. The application of such rigorous statistical procedures to explain the different sentencing patterns observed in Aboriginal and non-Aboriginal appearances is not appropriate here for several reasons: unlike the simple dichotomous outcomes of the two previous stages (arrest or non-arrest; Court referral or Aid Panel referral), here there are seven major penalty outcomes. In addition, the number of cases available for analysis was extremely small. Because penalties for the same offence varied from one place to another, it would have been necessary to limit analysis to young people resident in one area at the time of apprehension. Not only did this restrict the total number of Aboriginal cases available for analysis but also, of these only a very small proportion were sentenced to detention during the five-year study period; a number far too small to justify the application of rigorous statistical techniques. Hence, the approach adopted in the analysis of sentencing does no more than indicate which factors covary with and may therefore influence the differential Court outcomes for Aboriginal youth.

Notes

CHAPTER 1 Blacks and the Law

[1] An appearance is defined as one at which a final outcome is reached, thereby excluding all adjourned hearings in which no decision is finalised. Also, in this study, only initial, offence-related appearances have been considered. Consequential appearances relating to breach of bond applications, reconsideration of orders and discharge of bonds or recognisance are therefore omitted, as are all care-related matters. It should also be noted that appearances are not synonymous with individuals, since an individual may appear on more than one occasion during a given period. Hence, details such as the mode of apprehension, the nature and number of offence charges laid, the location of the hearing and the outcomes will be different from one appearance to another, even when the same person is involved. Since we are primarily concerned with the nature and outcome of each contact with the juvenile justice system, most of the analysis contained in this book relates to appearances.

CHAPTER 2 The Ideals of Juvenile Justice

[1] The essentials of the two models have been succinctly summarised by Freeman (1983: 82–6).

[2] These developments have been well documented elsewhere (Freeman, 1983: 68–9; Bruce, 1982: 5–12; McCabe and Treitel, 1983: 28–31).

[3] They are described in detail by Seymour (1983, Chapter 3) and their operation is analysed in Chapter 6 of this book.

CHAPTER 3 Welfare and Justice

[1] Delinquency was generally defined as 'those offences which have a subjective element affecting the character of the offender' (Adelaide Juvenile Court, *Annual Report 1962*: 1).

CHAPTER 4 Profile of the Aboriginal Young Offender

[1] The major charge is defined as the most serious offence charge brought in each appearance, with the maximum statutory penalty which could be imposed for a

given offence being used as the indicator of seriousness. Major charges for the 42,503 appearances which took place during the five-year study period were drawn from approximately 165 separate offence categories. To simplify discussion, we considered only those offences listed as the major charge in at least 0.5 per cent of all Aboriginal or, alternatively, all non-Aboriginal appearances. This procedure resulted in the selection of 26 offences which, in total, constituted the major charge in 94.9 per cent of the Aboriginal appearances and 91.7 per cent of the non-Aboriginal appearances.

[2] It should be stressed that this does not refer to all orders which may have been imposed on the youth over a number of years but only to those still in force at the time of the current appearance.

CHAPTER 5 Police: The Initiators of Justice?

[1] Although an appearance may involve multiple charges, our analysis focused only on the major charge; that is, the offence deemed to be the most serious one recorded for each appearance. The maximum statutory penalty which could be imposed was used to indicate the seriousness of any given offence.

[2] Prior to the matching process, all Aboriginal and non-Aboriginal appearances by Adelaide youths which contained one or more missing values for the variables of age, sex, address, family structure and occupation were discarded. This left 273 'useful' Aboriginal records for which matches were sought from some 5995 'useful' non-Aboriginal records.

[3] Whether or not the youth appeared as an absconder or under an existing order was excluded from the analysis because of the small numbers involved.

[4] It is worth noting, however, that although the numbers are far too small to be conclusive, the 92 Aboriginal and 92 non-Aboriginal appearances selected by this total matching process did not differ significantly in terms of the method of apprehension, with 33.7 per cent of the Aboriginal appearances being brought about by way of arrest compared with 27.2 per cent of the paired non-Aboriginal appearances. This suggests then, that in those very few cases where Aboriginal and non-Aboriginal youths resident in Adelaide came from the same socio-economic situations and possessed comparable offending profiles, the likelihood of arrest was approximately the same for both.

[5] Having already determined that the four legal variables each contributed to the arrest decision, it was stipulated that they could not be rejected during the logistic regression run. This considerably reduced the amount of computing space required and allowed all of the socio-economic and residential variables to be assessed by the step-wise procedure.

CHAPTER 6 Diversion or Trial: Who Decides?

[1] In Scotland, Children's Hearings replaced the Court system altogether, whereas in South Australia Aid Panels exist as an alternative to Court appearance.

[2] See also McCabe and Treitel (1983, p. 34ff).

[3] Theoretically challenge by prerogative writ is available, but there is no recorded instance of its exercise.

[4] A description of the statistical method involved and a detailed analysis of the results can be found in Gale and Wundersitz (1989).

Bibliography

Books, Articles and Reports

Adelaide Juvenile Court. *Twenty-Seventh Annual Report*, Year ended 30 June 1962, G.P.S., Adelaide.

Arnold, W.R., 1971. 'Race and ethnicity relative to other factors in Juvenile Court dispositions'. *American Journal of Sociology*, Vol. 77, No. 2, 211–27.

Axelrad, S., 1952. 'Negro and white institutionalised delinquents'. *American Journal of Sociology*, Vol. 57 (May), 569–74.

Baldwin, J., and Bottoms, A.E., 1976. *The Urban Criminal*. Tavistock, London.

Bennett, T.H., 1979. 'The social distribution of criminal labels'. *British Journal of Criminology*, Vol. 19, 134–45.

Bevan, O., 1984. 'Aborigines and police — Hostility, harmony or hopelessness?', *in* Swanton, B. (ed.), *Aborigines and Criminal Justice*, Australian Institute of Criminology, Canberra, 107–11.

Biles, D., 1988. *Research into Aboriginal Deaths in Custody*. Paper presented to the Fourth Annual Conference of the Australian and New Zealand Society of Criminology, 22–24 August 1988, Uni. of Sydney.

Brady, M., and Morice, R., 1982. *Aboriginal Adolescent Offending Behaviour: A Study of a Remote Community*. Western Desert Project, School of Medicine, Flinders Uni. of S.A.

Broadhurst, R.G., Maller, R.A., Maller, M.G., and Duffecy, J., 1988. 'Aboriginal and non-Aboriginal recidivism in Western Australia: A failure rate analysis'. *Journal of Research in Crime and Delinquency*, Vol. 25, No. 1, 83–108.

Bruce, N., 1982. 'The Children's Hearings System: Historical background', Chapter 1, *in* Martin, F.M., and Murray, K. (eds), *The Scottish Juvenile Justice System*, Scottish Academic Press, Edinburgh.

Bullock, H., 1961. 'Significance of the racial factor in the length of prison sentences'. *Journal of Criminal Law, Criminology and Police Science*, Vol. 52, 411–17.

Burke, P.J., and Turk, A.T., 1975. 'Factors affecting post-arrest dispositions: A model for analysis'. *Social Problems*, Vol. 22 (February), 313–32.

Chambliss, W.J., and Nagasawa, R.H., 1969. 'On the validity of official statistics: A comparative study of white, black and Japanese high-school boys'. *Journal of Research in Crime and Delinquency*, Vol. 6, 71–7.

Chapman, D.J., 1976. 'Sentencing Aborigines: The Port Adelaide Magistrate's Court'. *Legal Service Bulletin*, Vol. 2, No. 4, 131–2.

Chilton, R., and Galvin, J., 1985. 'Race, crime and criminal justice'. *Crime and Delinquency*, Vol. 31, No. 1, 3–14.

Chiricos, T.G., Jackson, P.D., and Waldo, G.P., 1972. 'Inequality in the imposition of a criminal label'. *Social Problems*, Vol. 19, 553–72.

Chiricos, T.G., and Waldo, G.P., 1975. 'Socio-economic status and criminal sentencing: An empirical assessment of a conflict proposition'. *American Sociological Review*, Vol. 40 (December), 753–72.

Chisholm, R., 1983. 'Aboriginal Children Before the Courts: A Study of Bourke and Nowra', mimeo.

Chused, R.H., 1973. 'The Juvenile Court process: A study of three New Jersey counties'. *Rutger's Law Review*, Vol. 26, 488–539.

Clifford, W., 1981. *Aboriginal Criminological Research: Report of a Workshop held 3–4 March 1981*. Australian Institute of Criminology, Canberra.

Cohen, L.E., 1975. *Delinquency Dispositions: An Empirical Analysis of Processing Decisions in Three Juvenile Courts*. U.S. Dept of Justice, National Criminal Justice Information and Statistical Service, No. SD-AR-9, Govt Printing Office, Washington D.C.

Cohen, L.E., and Kluegel, J.R., 1978. 'Determinants of Juvenile Court dispositions: Ascriptive and achieved factors in two metropolitan courts'. *American Sociological Review*, Vol. 43 (April), 162–78.

Collett, A.C., and Graves, A.A., 1972. 'A Study of the Nature and Origin of Aboriginal Petty Crime in Port Augusta', mimeo.

Crow, I., 1987. 'Black people and criminal justice in the U.K.'. *The Howard Journal*, Vol. 26, No. 4, 303–13.

Crow, I., and Cove, J., 1984. 'Ethnic minorities and the courts'. *Criminal Law Review*, 413–17.

Cunneen, C., and Robb, T., 1987. *Criminal Justice in North-West N.S.W.* N.S.W. Bureau of Crime Statistics and Research, Attorney-General's Dept, Sydney.

Dannefer, D., and Schutt, R.K., 1982. 'Race and juvenile justice processing in Court and police agencies'. *American Journal of Sociology*, Vol. 87, No. 5, 1113–32.

Department of Community Welfare Services (Vic.), 1982. *Characteristics of Young People in Youth Training Centres: Results of the Youth Training Centre Census 1982 and Trends Over the Previous Decades*. Office of Research and Social Policy, Dept of Community Welfare Services, Victoria.

Department for Community Services (W.A.), 1982. *An initial and supplementary report on a study of children who enter the care of the Department for Community Services and are subsequently admitted to an adult penal facility before the ages of 20 and 22 years*. Perth.

Department of the Attorney-General (S.A.), Office of Crime Statistics, 1982. *Statistics from Courts of Summary Jurisdiction, Selected Returns from Adelaide Magistrate's Court, 1979–82*. Adelaide.

Department of the Attorney-General (S.A.), Office of Crime Statistics, 1981. *Crime and Justice in South Australia*, Series A. Adelaide.

Eggleston, E., 1976. *Fear, Favour and Affection: Aborigines and the Criminal Law in Victoria, South Australia and Western Australia*. A.N.U. Press, Canberra.

Elion, V.H., and Megargee, E.I., 1979. 'Racial identity, length of incarceration and parole decision-making'. *Journal of Research in Crime and Delinquency*, July, 232–45.

Farnworth, M., and Horan, P.M., 1978. *Race Differences in the Processing of Criminal Defendants*. Paper presented at Southern Sociological Society Meeting, New Orleans.

Farrington, D.P., and Bennett, T., 1981. 'Police cautioning of juveniles in London'. *British Journal of Criminology*, Vol. 21, 123–35.

Feeley, M., 1979. *The Process is the Punishment*. Russell Sage Foundation, New York.

Foley, M., 1982. 'Research in Aboriginal and Islander Child Welfare'. Paper presented to seminar on Aboriginal and Islander Child Welfare.

Freeman, M. A., 1983. *The Rights and Wrongs of Children*. Frances Pinter, London.

Gale, F., 1972. *Urban Aborigines*. A.N.U. Press, Canberra.

Gale, F., and Wundersitz, J., 1982. *Adelaide Aborigines: A Case Study of Urban Life, 1966–1981*. Development Studies Centre, A.N.U., Canberra.

Gale, F., and Wundersitz, J., 1989. 'The operation of hidden prejudice in pre-Court procedures: the case of Australian Aboriginal youth'. *Australian and New Zealand Journal of Criminology*, Vol. 22, No. 1, 1–21.

Gilroy, M., 1976. 'Youthful offenders at Groote Eylandt'. *Legal Service Bulletin*, Vol. 2, No. 4, 124–6.

Gold, M., and Reimer, D.J., 1975. 'Changing patterns of delinquent behaviour among Americans 13 through 16 years old: 1967–1972'. *Crime and Delinquency Literature*, Vol. 7, 483–517.

Goldman, N., 1963. *The Differential Selection of Juvenile Offenders for Court Appearance*. National Council on Crime and Delinquency, New York.

Green, E., 1964. 'Inter- and intra-racial crime relative to sentencing'. *Journal of Criminal Law, Criminology and Police Science*, Vol. 55, 348–58.

Hagan, J., 1974. 'Extra-legal attributes and criminal sentencing: An assessment of a sociological viewpoint'. *Law and Society Review*, Vol. 8, No. 3, 357–83.

Hagan, J., 1975. 'The social and legal construction of criminal justice: A study of the pre-sentence process'. *Social Problems*, Vol. 11 (June), 620–37.

Hanks, P., and Keon-Cohen, B. (eds), 1984. *Aborigines and the Law*. Allen and Unwin, Sydney.

Harding, R., 1985. 'Opening Address', in Hazlehurst, K.M. (ed.), *Justice Programs for Aboriginal and Other Indigenous Communities: Australia, New Zealand, Canada, Fiji, Papua New Guinea*. Seminar Proceedings No. 7, Australian Institute of Criminology, Canberra.

Harries, K.P., 1980. *Crime and the Environment*. Charles C. Thomas, Springfield, Illinois.

Hazlehurst, K.M. (ed.), 1985. *Justice Programs for Aboriginal and Other Indigenous Communities: Australia, New Zealand, Canada, Fiji, Papua New Guinea*. Seminar Proceedings No. 7, Australian Institute of Criminology, Canberra.

Hazlehurst, K.M. (ed.), 1987. *Ivory Scales: Black Australia and the Law*. N.S.W. University Press, in association with the Australian Institute of Criminology, Sydney.

Hepburn, J.R., 1978. 'Race and the decision to arrest: An analysis of warrants issued'. *Journal of Research in Crime and Delinquency*, January, 54–73.

Herbert, D.T., 1982. *The Geography of Urban Crime*. Longman, London.

Hirschi, T., 1969. *Causes of Delinquency*. Berkeley, University of California Press.

Landau, S.F., 1981. 'Juveniles and the police: Who is charged immediately and who is referred to the Juvenile Bureau?'. *British Journal of Criminology*, Vol. 21, No. 1, 27–46.

Landau, S.F., and Nathan, G., 1983. 'Selecting delinquents for cautioning in the London Metropolitan Area'. *British Journal of Criminology*, Vol. 23, No. 2, 128–149.

Ligertwood, A., 1984. 'Aborigines in the criminal courts', *in* Hanks, P., and Keon-Cohen, B. (eds), *Aborigines and the Law*, Allen and Unwin, Sydney, 191–211.

Lizotte, A.J., 1978. 'Extra-legal factors in Chicago's criminal courts: Testing the conflict model of criminal justice'. *Social Problems*, June, 564–80.

Lockyer, 1982. 'Justice and welfare', Chapter 14, *in* Martin, F.M., and Murray, K. (eds), *The Scottish Juvenile Justice System*, Scottish Academic Press, Edinburgh.

Lyons, G., 1983. 'Aboriginal perceptions of courts and police: A Victorian study'. *Australian Aboriginal Studies*, No. 2, 45–61.

McCabe, S., and Treitel, P., 1983. *Juvenile Justice in the United Kingdom: Comparisons and Suggestions for Change*. New Approaches to Juvenile Crime, London.

McConville, M., and Baldwin, J., 1982. 'The influence of race on sentencing in England'. *Criminal Law Review*, 652–8.

McCorquodale, J.C., 1980. 'Aborigines and alcohol: A study of five "Aboriginal towns" in New South Wales', *in Aborigines and the Criminal Law*, University of Sydney, Proceedings of the Institute of Criminology, No. 44, 48–60.

Martin, F.M., 1982. 'Theories of delinquency', Chapter 11, *in* Martin, F.M., and Murray, K. (eds), *The Scottish Juvenile Justice System*, Scottish Academic Press, Edinburgh.

Martin, F.M., and Murray, F. (eds), 1982. *The Scottish Juvenile Justice System*. Scottish Academic Press, Edinburgh.

Martin, M., and Newby, L., 1984. 'Aborigines in Summary Courts in Western Australia, a regional study: Preliminary report on selected findings', *in* Swanton, B. (ed.), *Aborigines and Criminal Justice*, Australian Institute of Criminology, Canberra, 295–305.

Mildern, E.J., 1973. 'The Western Australian Juvenile Suspended Action Panel: A Baseline Study'. Unpublished Master of Social Work thesis, University of Western Australia.

Milne, C., 1982. *Aboriginal Children in Substitute Care, July 1982*. Aboriginal Children's Research Project, Family and Children's Services Agency, Sydney.

Milne, T., 1983. 'Aborigines and the criminal justice system', *in* Findlay, M., Egger, S.J., and Sutton, J. (eds), *Issues in Criminal Justice Administration*, Allen and Unwin, Sydney, 184–99.

Mohr, J., 1977. *Report of the Royal Commission into the Administration of the Juvenile Courts Act and Other Associated Matters*. South Australian Government Printer, Adelaide.

Mott, J., 1983. 'Police decisions for dealing with juvenile offenders'. *British Journal of Criminology*, Vol. 23, No. 3, 249–62.

Muirhead, J., 1989. *Interim Report of the Royal Commission into Black Deaths in Custody*. A.G.P.S., Canberra.

Murray, J., 1985. 'The development of contemporary juvenile justice and correctional policy', in Borowski, A., and Murray, J.M. (eds), *Juvenile Delinquency in Australia*, Methuen, Sydney, 68–92.

Newman, L.K., 1983. 'Juvenile justice in South Australia', in Children's Court Advisory Committee, *Annual Report 1983*, S.A.G.P., Adelaide.

Nichols, H., 1985. 'Children's Aid Panels in South Australia', in Borowski, A., and Murray, J.M. (eds), *Juvenile Delinquency in Australia*, Methuen, Sydney, 221–35.

Parker, G., 1976. 'The Juvenile Court Movement'. *University of Toronto Law Journal*, Vol. 26, 140–72.

Pathe, Mark, 1985. 'Police–Aboriginal relations in South Australia', in Hazlehurst, K.M. (ed.), *Justice Programs for Aboriginal and Other Indigenous Communities: Australia, New Zealand, Canada, Fiji and Papua New Guinea*, Seminar Proceedings No. 7, Australian Institute of Criminology, Canberra.

Penniall, W., 1982. *Children in Care in N.S.W., 1982*. Youth and Community Services, Sydney.

Petersen, D., and Friday, P., 1975. 'Early release from incarceration: Race as a factor in the use of shock probation'. *Journal of Criminal Law and Criminology*, March, 79–87.

Petersen, R.D., and Hagan, J., 1984. 'Changing conceptions of race: Towards an account of anomalous findings on sentencing research'. *American Sociological Review*, Vol. 49, 56–70.

'Police–Aboriginal Relations Discussion Paper', 1984, unpublished paper, Adelaide, S.A.

Pope, C.E., 1978. 'Post-arrest release decisions: An empirical examination of social and legal criteria'. *Journal of Research in Crime and Delinquency*, January, 35–53.

Pope, C.E., 1979. 'Race and crime revisited'. *Journal of Research in Crime and Delinquency*, July, 347–57.

President's Commission on Law Enforcement and Justice, *Report: Juvenile Delinquency and Youth Crime*, 1967. Washington, U.S.A.

Priestley, P., Fears, D., and Fuller, R., 1977. *Justice for Juveniles*. Routledge and Kegan Paul, London.

Pyle, G.F., 1974. *The Spatial Dynamics of Crime*. University of Chicago, Dept of Geography, Research Paper No. 159, Chicago.

Royal Commission into the Administration of the Juvenile Courts Act and Other Associated Matters: see Mohr, J., 1977.

Royal Commission into Black Deaths in Custody: see Muirhead, J., 1989.

Ruddock, P.M., 1980. *Aboriginal Legal Aid*. House of Representatives Standing Committee on Aboriginal Affairs, A.G.P.S., Canberra.

Sarri, R. and Bradley, R.W., 1980. 'Juvenile Aid Panels: An alternative to Juvenile Court processing in South Australia'. *Journal of Research in Crime and Delinquency*, 42–62.

Seymour, J., 1983. *Juvenile Justice in South Australia*. Law Book Co., Sydney.

Sinclair, A., 1982. 'The Children's Hearings System: Entering the system', Chapter 3 in Martin, J.M., and Murray, K. (eds), *The Scottish Juvenile Justice System*, Scottish Academic Press, Edinburgh.

Social Welfare Advisory Council (S.A.), 1968. *Report on the Establishment of a Juvenile Crime Prevention Scheme*. Adelaide, S.A.

Social Welfare Advisory Council (S.A.), 1970. *Report on the Legislation Concerning Juvenile Offenders*. Adelaide, S.A.

Stevens, P., and Willis, C.F., 1979. *Race, Crime and Arrests*. Home Office Research Study No. 58, Her Majesty's Stationary Office, London.

Sutton, A., and Koshnitsky, N., 1983. 'The value of crime statistics: Counting crime'. *Legal Service Bulletin*, 62–4.

Swanton, B. (ed.), 1984. *Aborigines and Criminal Justice*, Australian Institute of Criminology, Canberra.

Taft, R., 1970. 'Attitudes of Western Australians towards Aborigines', *in* Taft, R., Dawson, J., and Beasley, P., *Attitudes and Social Conditions*, A.N.U. Press, Canberra, 3–72.

Terry, R.M., 1967. 'The screening of juvenile offenders'. *Journal of Criminal Law, Criminology and Police Science*, Vol. 58, 173–81.

Thomas, R.J., and Zingraff, M.T., 1981. 'Detecting sentencing disparity: Some problems and evidence'. *American Journal of Sociology*, Vol. 86, 869–80.

Thornberry, T.P., 1973. 'Race, socio-economic status and sentencing in the juvenile justice system'. *Journal of Criminal Law, Criminology and Police Science*, Vol. 64 (March), 90–8.

Wellford, C., 1975. 'Labelling Theory and criminology: An assessment'. *Social Problems*, Vol. 22 (February), 332–45.

Western, J.S., 1969. 'The Australian Aborigine: What white Australians know and think about them — a preliminary survey'. *Race*, Vol. 10, No. 4, 411–34.

Williams, J.R., and Gold, M., 1972. 'From delinquent behaviour to official delinquency'. *Social Problems*, Vol. 20, 209–29.

Wolfgang, M.E., Figlio, R.M., and Sellin, T., 1972. *Delinquency in a Birth Cohort*. University of Chicago Press, Chicago.

Wundersitz, J., 1979a. 'White Attitudes Towards Aborigines: A Study'. *Proceedings of Royal Geographical Society of Australasia, South Australian Branch*, Vol. 18, 70–76.

Wundersitz, J., 1979b. 'A Study of White Attitudes Towards Aborigines in the Maitland and Port Victoria District of Central Yorke Peninsula'. Unpublished M.A. thesis, The University of Adelaide.

Cases

Re Gault (1967), 387 U.S. 1.
Hallam v. *O'Dea* (1979), 22 S.A.S.R. 136.
R. v. *S., V. and Nates* (1982), 31 S.A.S.R. 266.

Statutes

Child Welfare Amendment Act 1978 *(W.A.)*.
Children and Young Persons Act 1969 *(U.K.)*.
Children's Protection and Young Offenders Act 1979 *(S.A.)*.
Children's Protection and Young Offenders Act Amendment Act 1988 *(S.A.)*.
Juvenile Courts Act 1941 *(S.A.)*.
Juvenile Courts Act 1965 *(S.A.)*.
Juvenile Courts Act 1971 *(S.A.)*.
Minor Offences Act 1869 *(S.A.)*.
Social Work (Scotland) Act 1968 *(U.K.)*.
State Children's Act 1895 *(S.A.)*.
Summary Procedure Act 1847 *(U.K.)*.

Index

Lightning Source UK Ltd.
Milton Keynes UK
UKHW010309111218
333800UK00001B/27/P